Learn & Color
STAINED GLASS SERIES
Landscapes & Seascapes

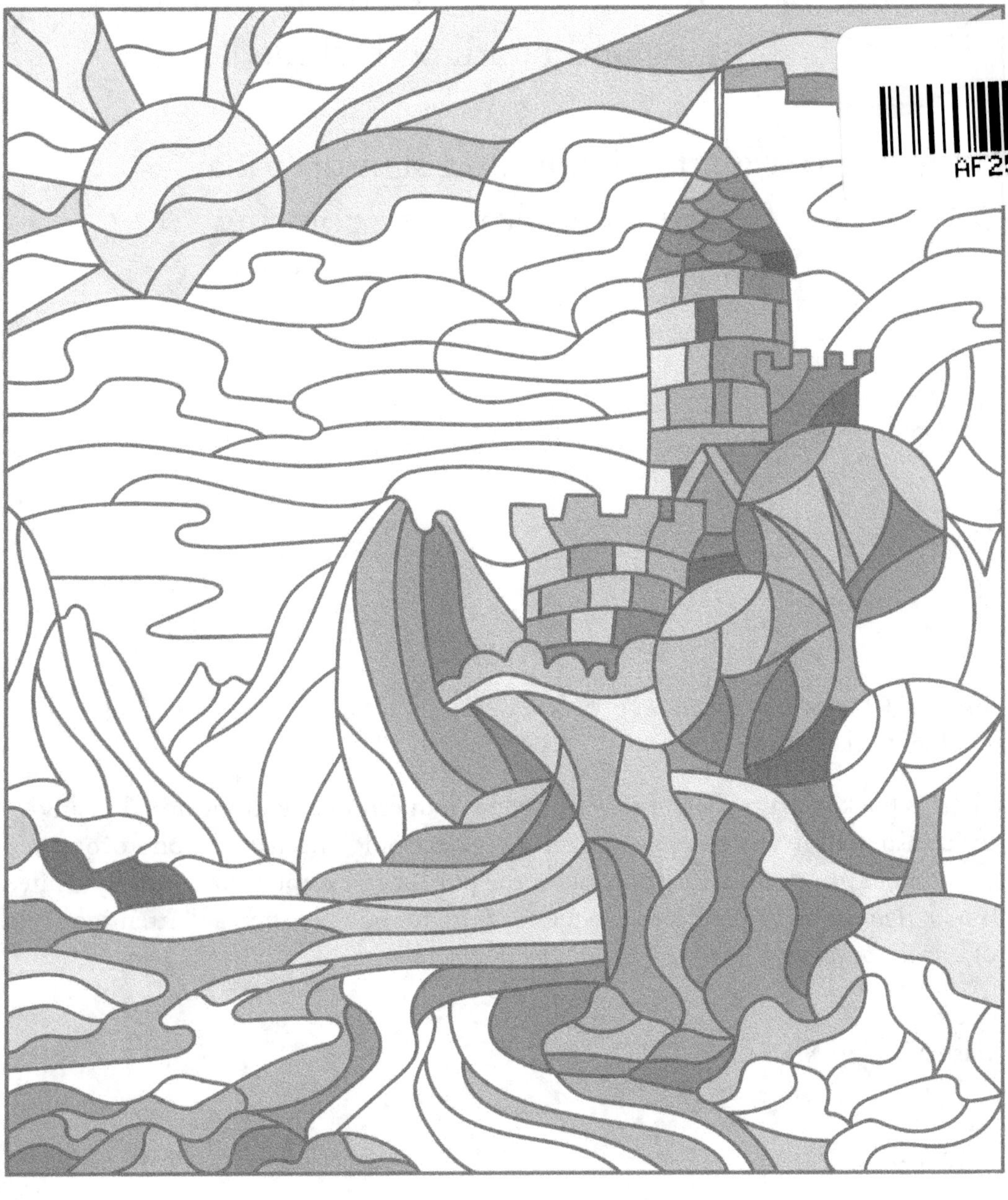

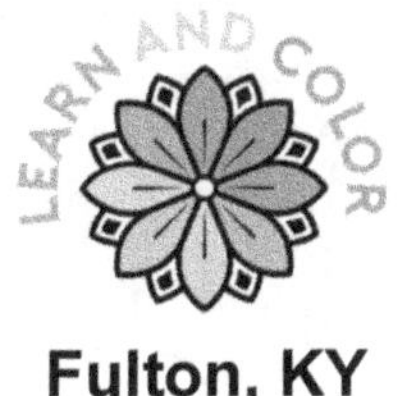

Fulton, KY

Subscribe and Save

We offer a new way for you to receive more and more coloring books at a significant savings through our subscription option.

Each month your next coloring book can be delivered right to your mail box. You'll receive a discount from the retail price with shipping and handling included!

Find out all the details and sign up today
http://LearnAndColor.com/coloring

Learn and Color Stained Glass Series – Landscapes & Seascapes
© 2018 Master Design Marketing, LLC

All rights reserved. This book or parts thereof may not be reproduced in any form, stored in any retrieval system, or transmitted in any form by any means—electronic, mechanical, photocopy, recording, or otherwise—without prior written permission of the publisher, except as provided by United States of America copyright law. For permission requests, write to the publisher, at "Attention: Permissions Coordinator," at the address below.

Learn & Color Books
  an imprint of Master Design Marketing, LLC
  789 State Route 94 E
  Fulton, KY 42041
  www.LearnAndColor.com

For information about special discounts available for bulk purchases, sales promotions, fund-raising and educational needs, contact Learn & Color Books Company Sales at sales@LearnAndColor.com.

ISBN 978-1-947482-08-1

Cover design by Faithe F Thomas
All images in this book are by Natalia Zagory © 123RF
Look for the Scottish Flag somewhere in each of our books.

Sample Pages from
Landscapes & Seascapes

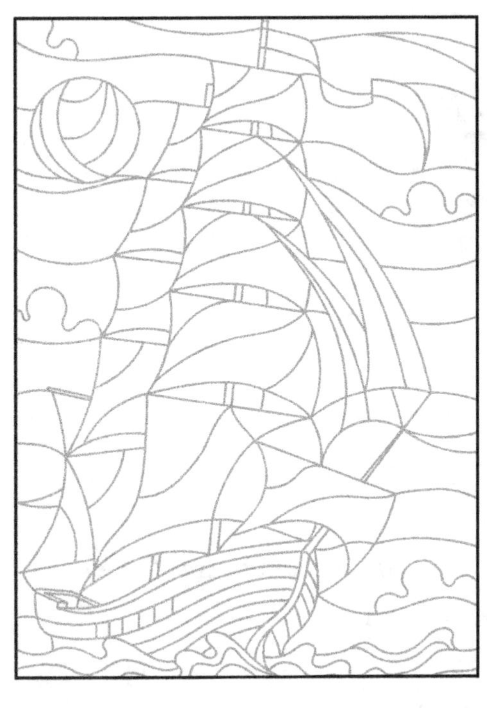

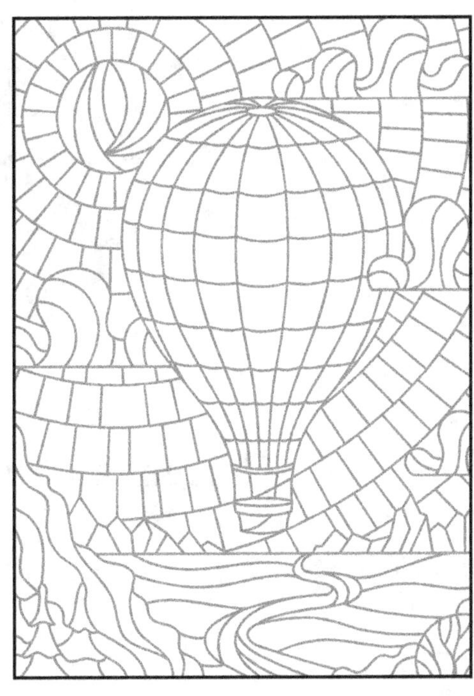

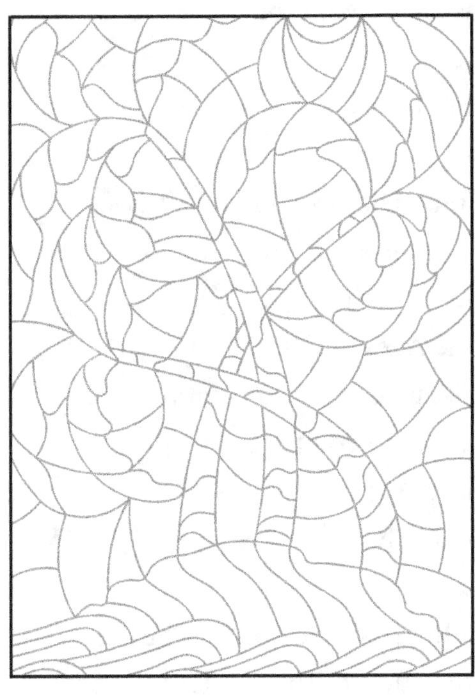

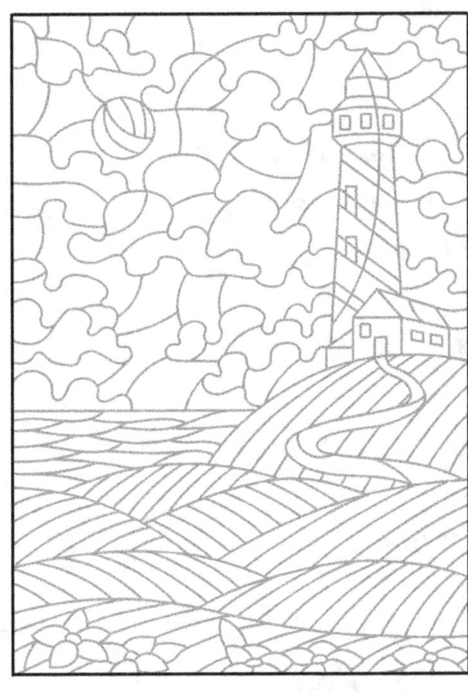

Enjoy other books by

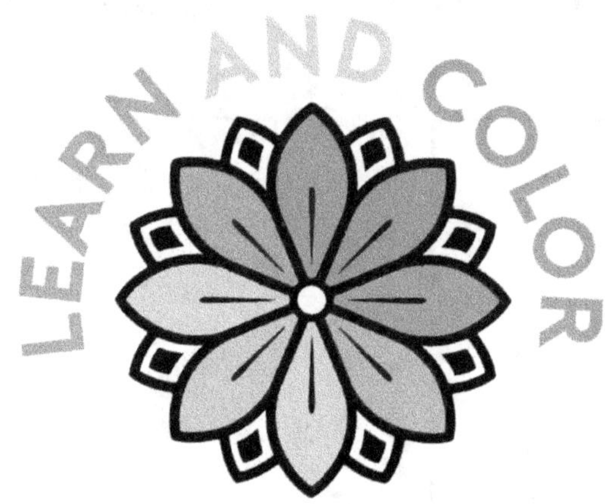

Current and upcoming titles:

Learn and Color Nature Series

Medicinal Herbs

Freshwater Fish

Garden Plants

Trees

Bugs and Insects

Fossils

Learn and Color Stained Glass Series

Landscapes & Seascapes

Fish & Fowl

Flowers

Birds, Bees, & Butterflies

Animals

Designs

Sea Creatures

Christian Images

Learn and Color the Bible Series

Promises   Places

Prayers   Psalms

Proverbs   People

Learn and Color Historical Figures Series

Early Civilization

The Ancient World

The Middle Ages

The Renaissance and Reformation

The Industrial Revolution

The Modern Age

The Present Day

Learn and Color Historical Events Series

Early Civilization

The Ancient World

The Middle Ages

The Renaissance and Reformation

The Industrial Revolution

The Modern Age

The Present Day

Learn and Color Historical Places Series

Early Civilization & The Ancient World

The Middle Ages, Renaissance, & Reformation

The Modern Age

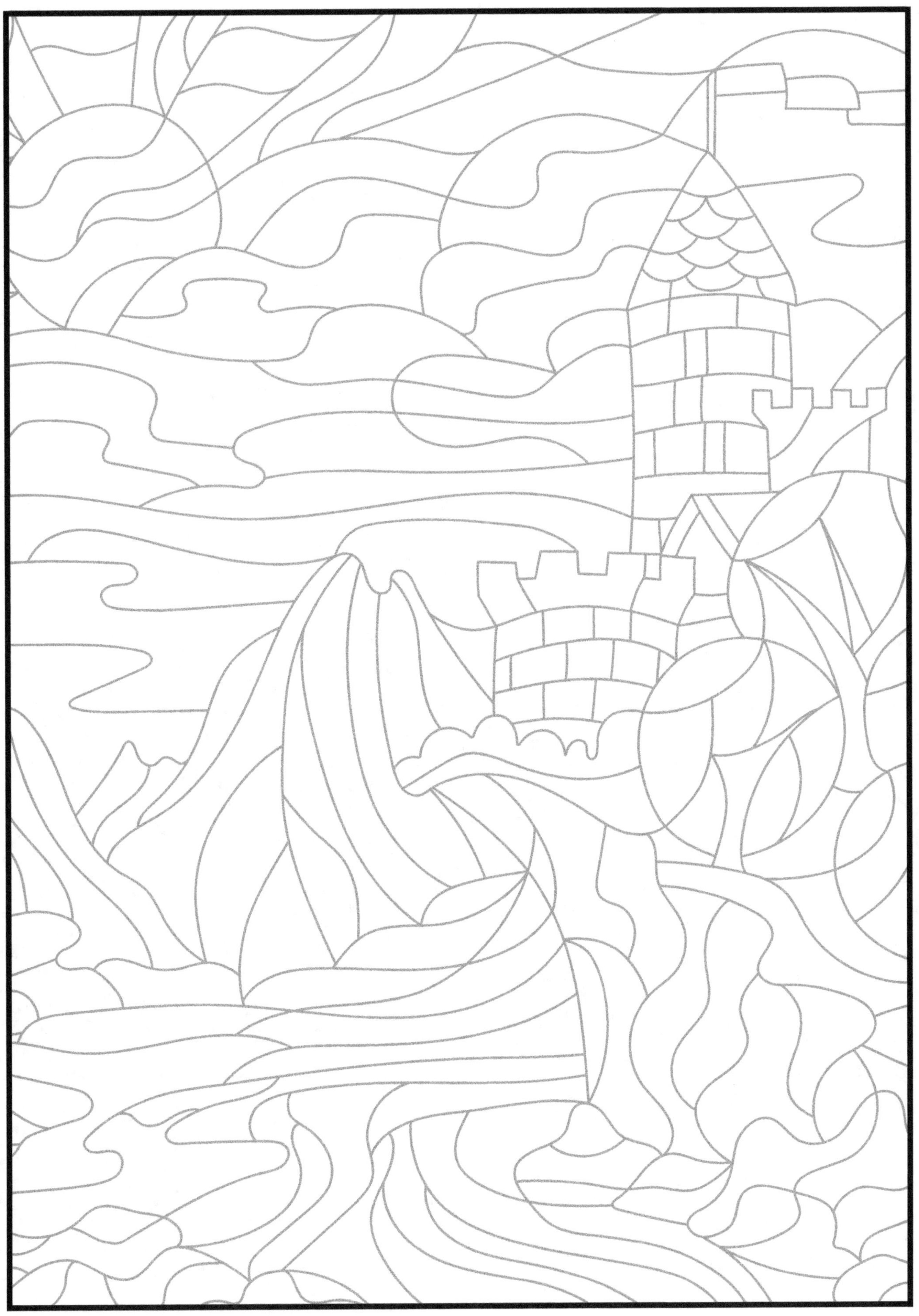

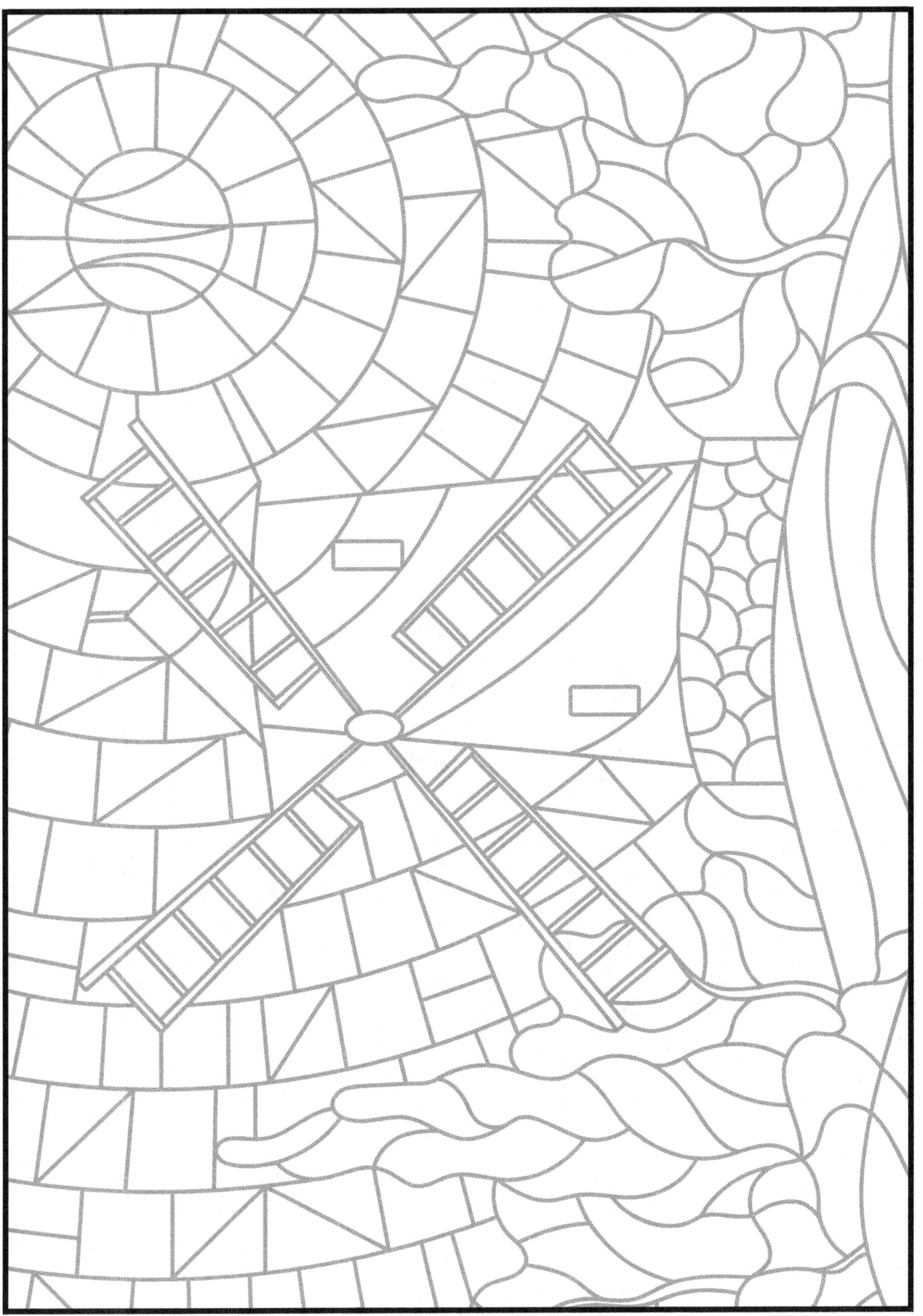

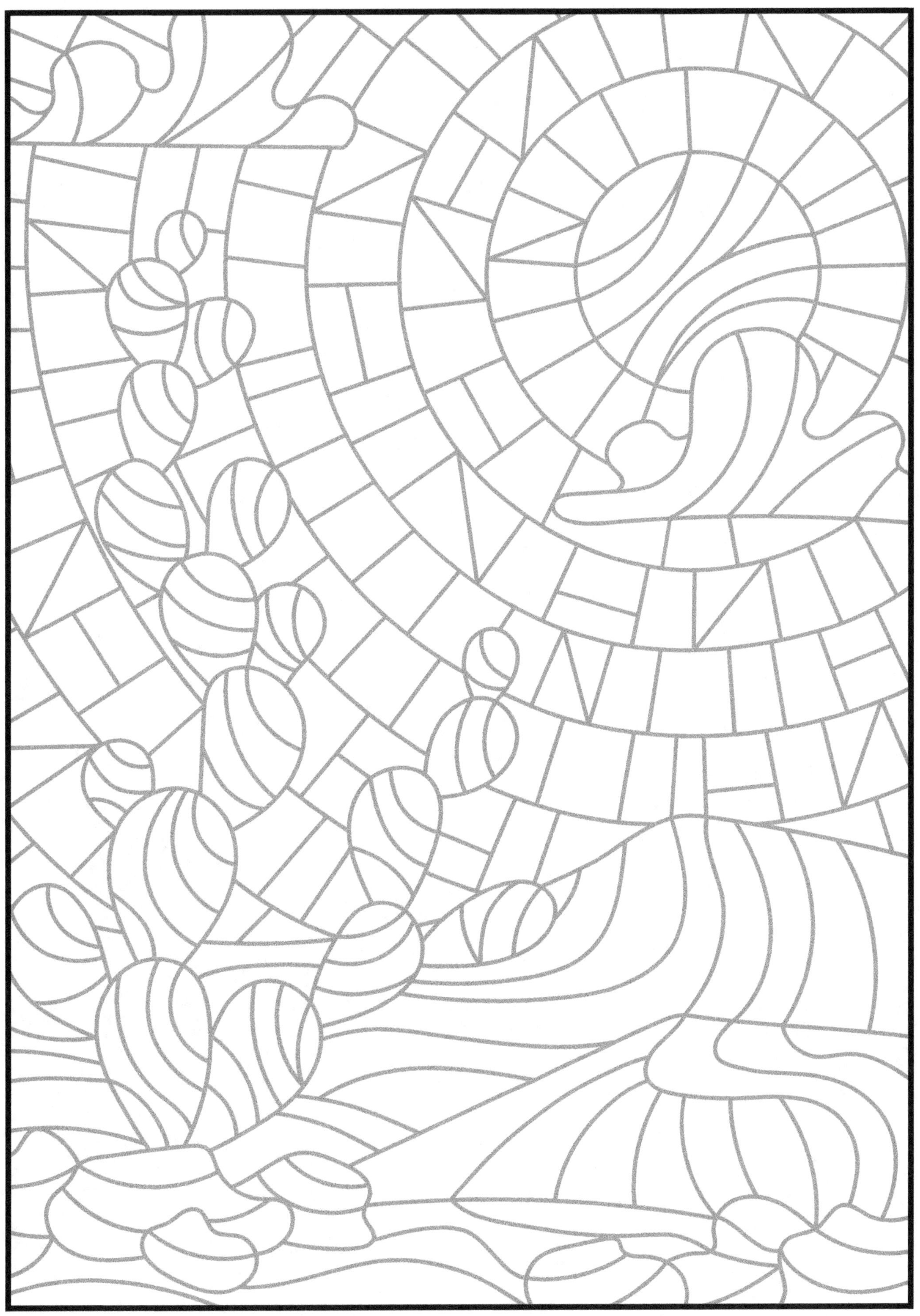

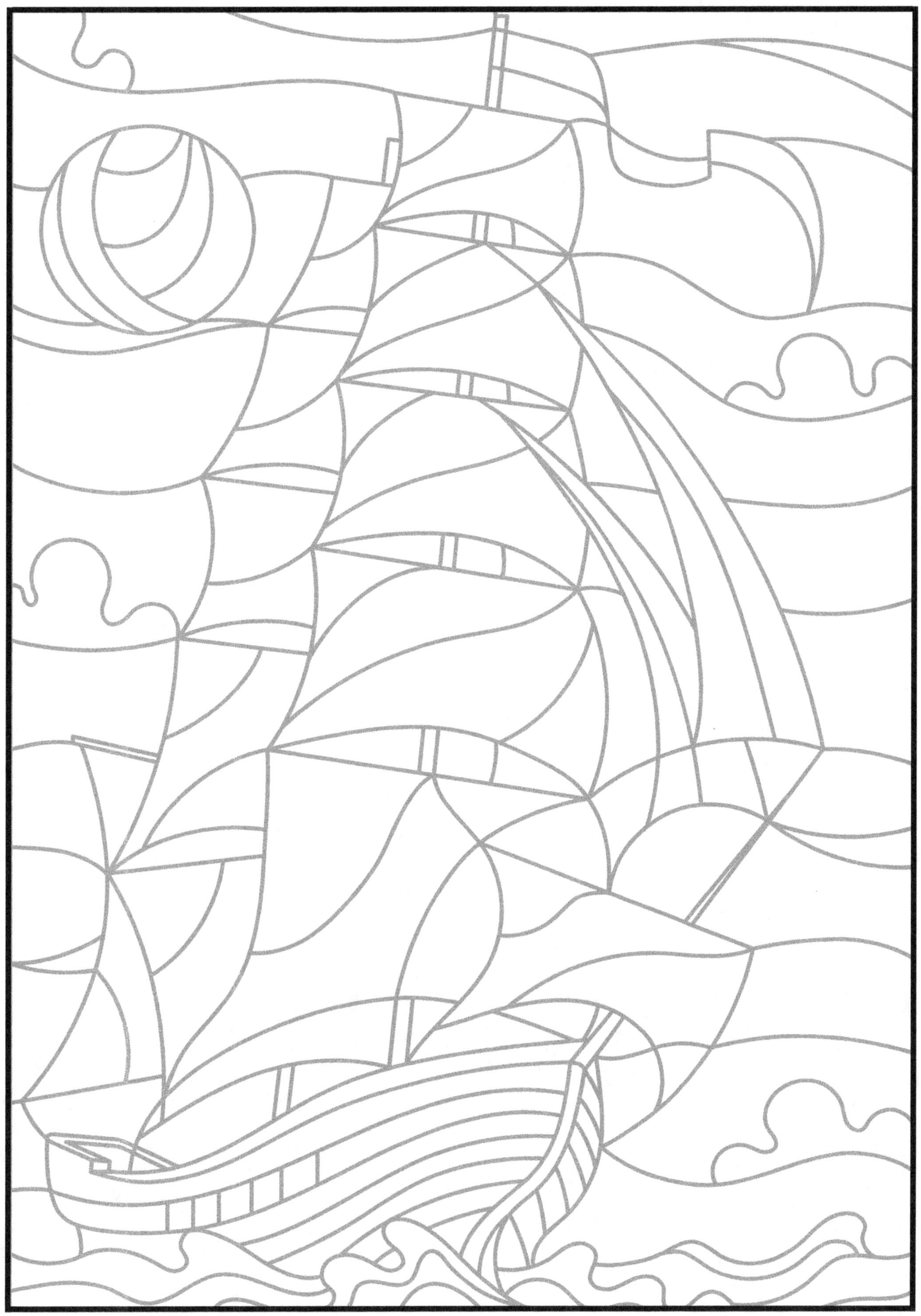

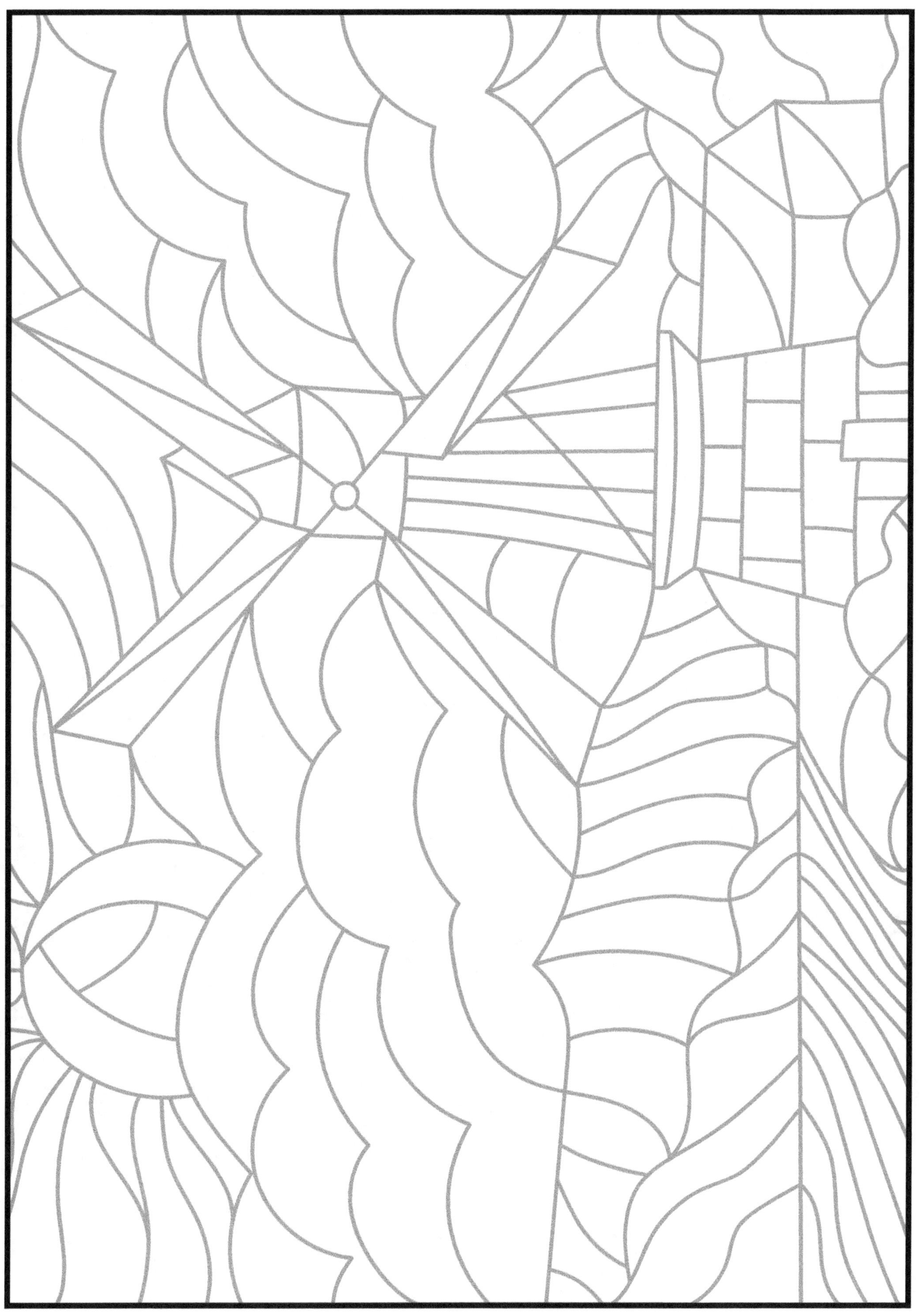

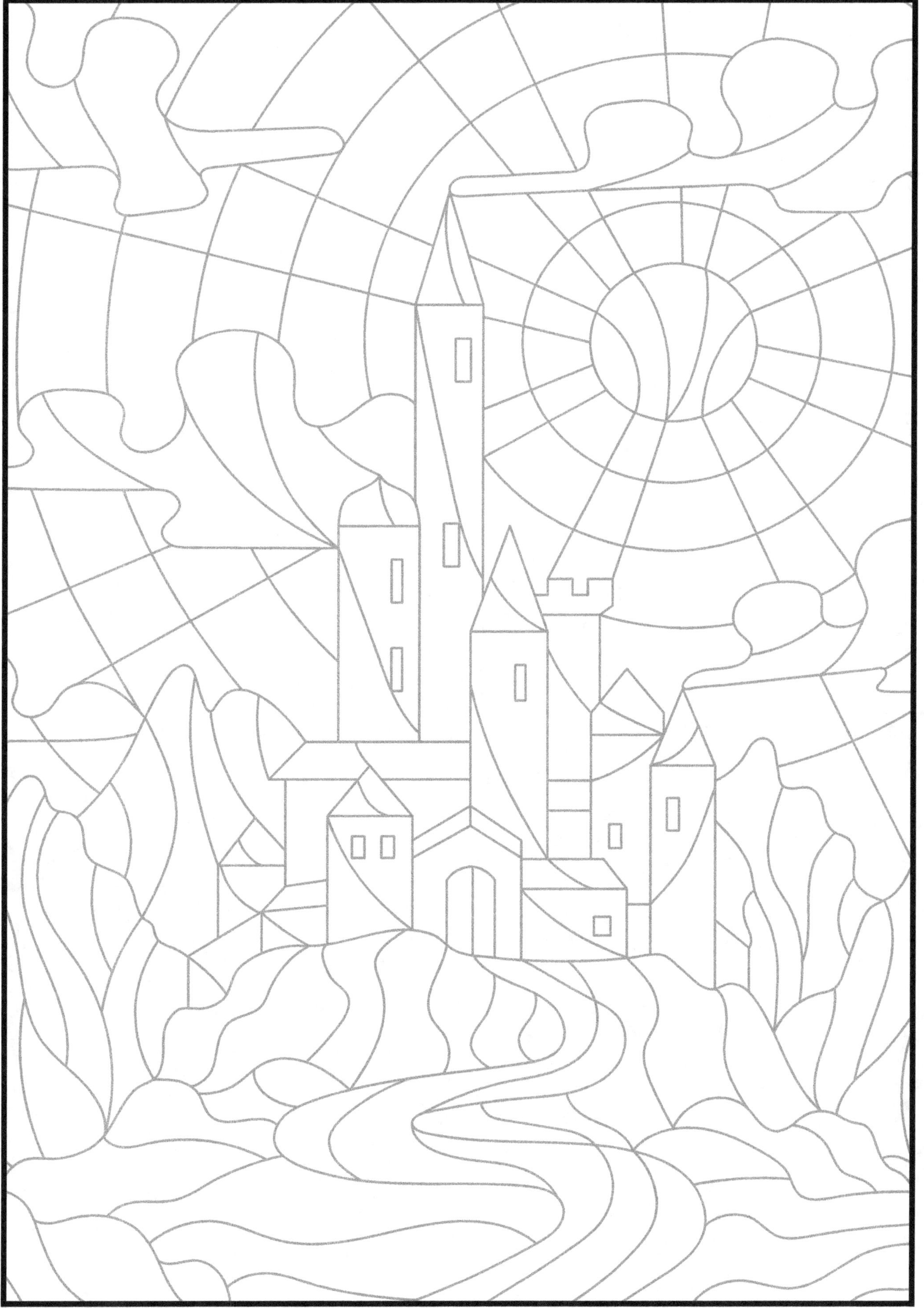

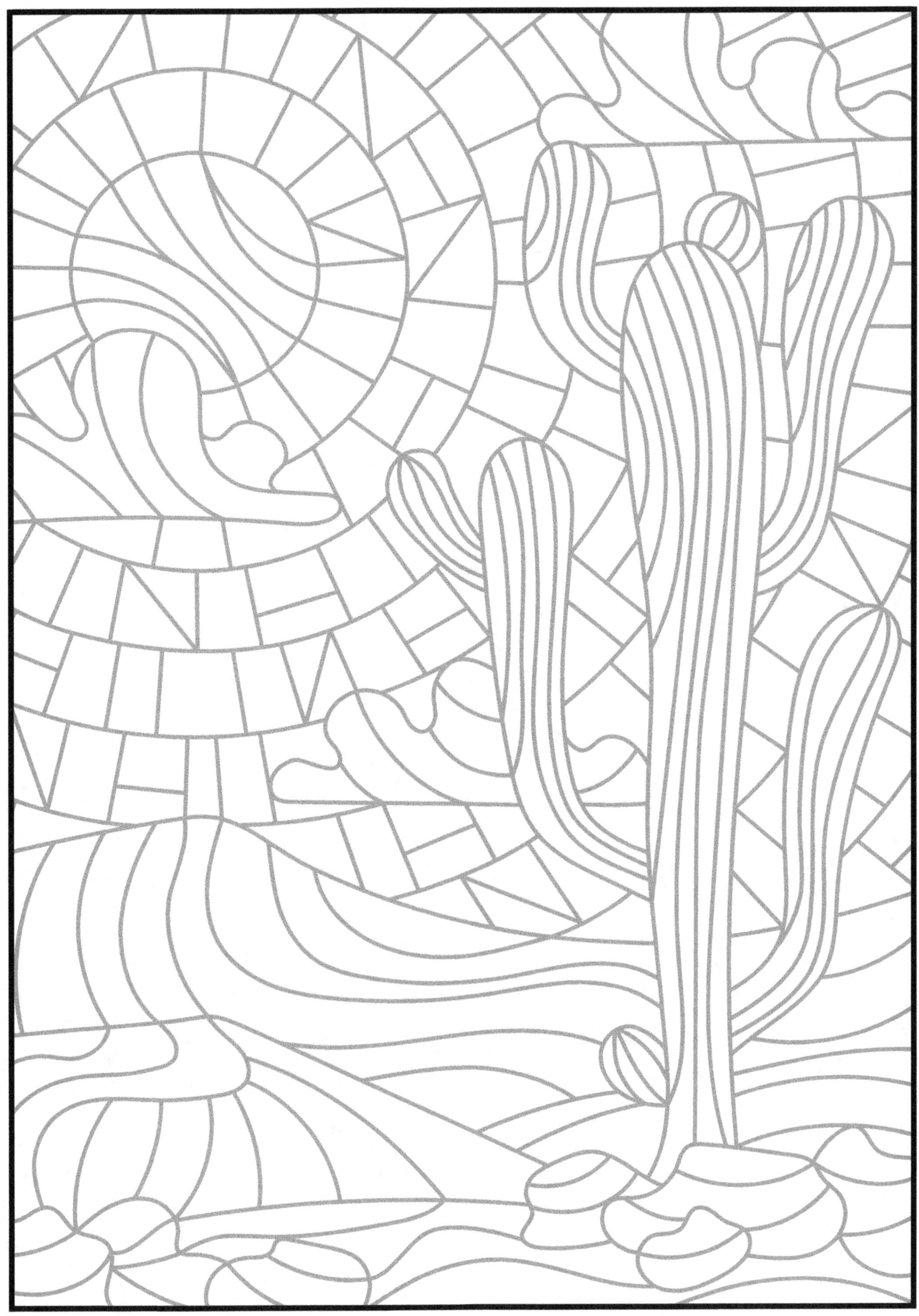

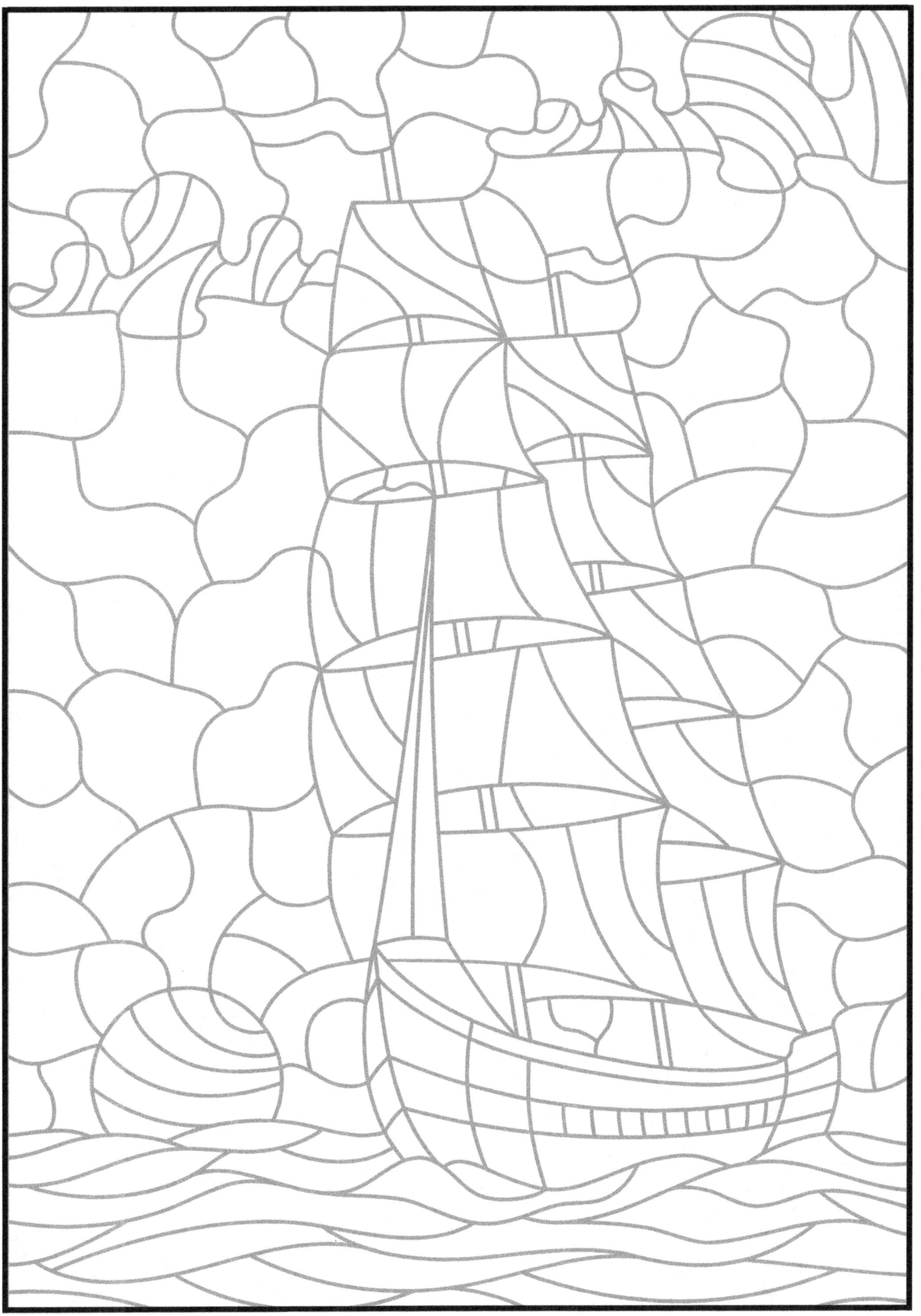

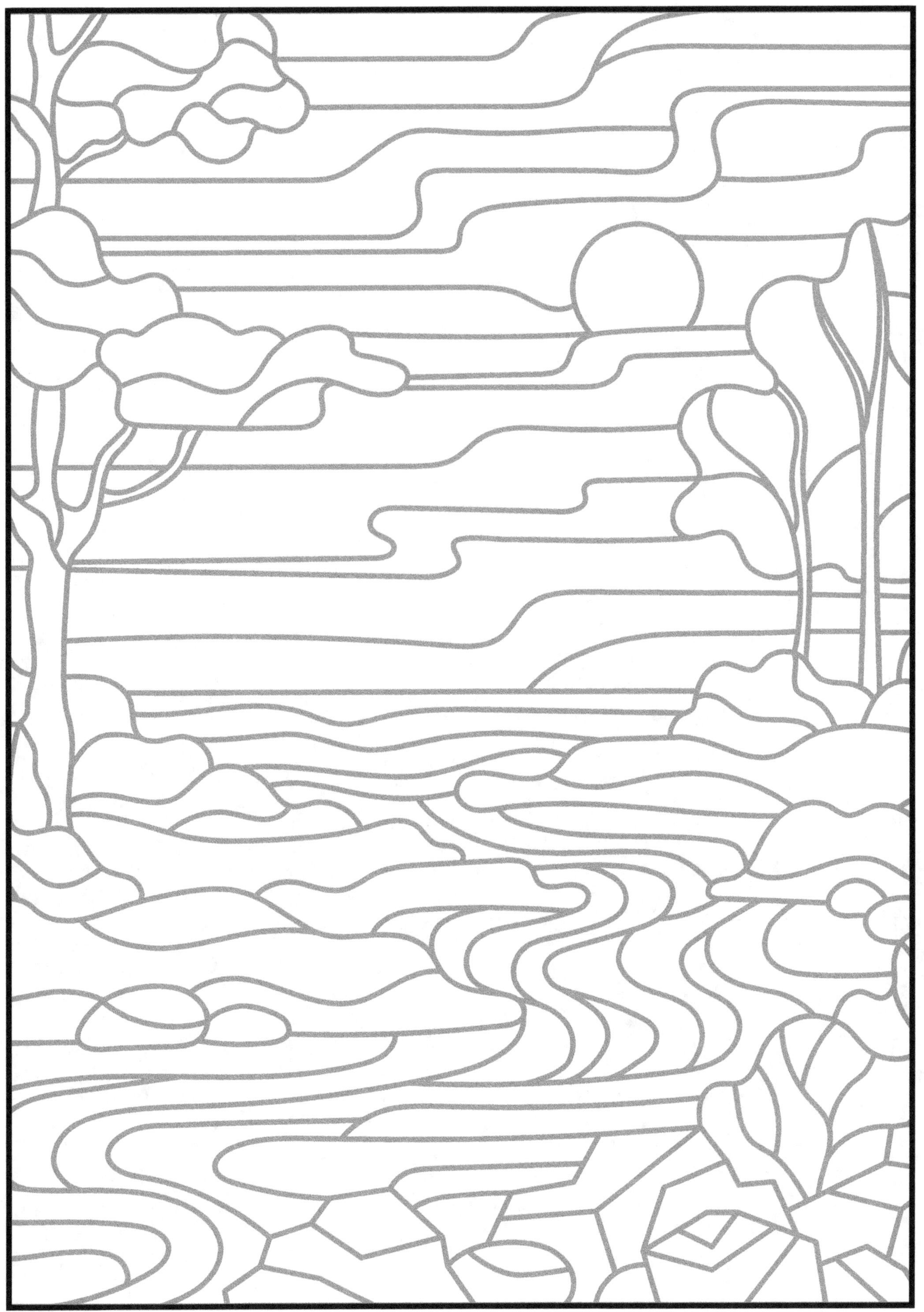

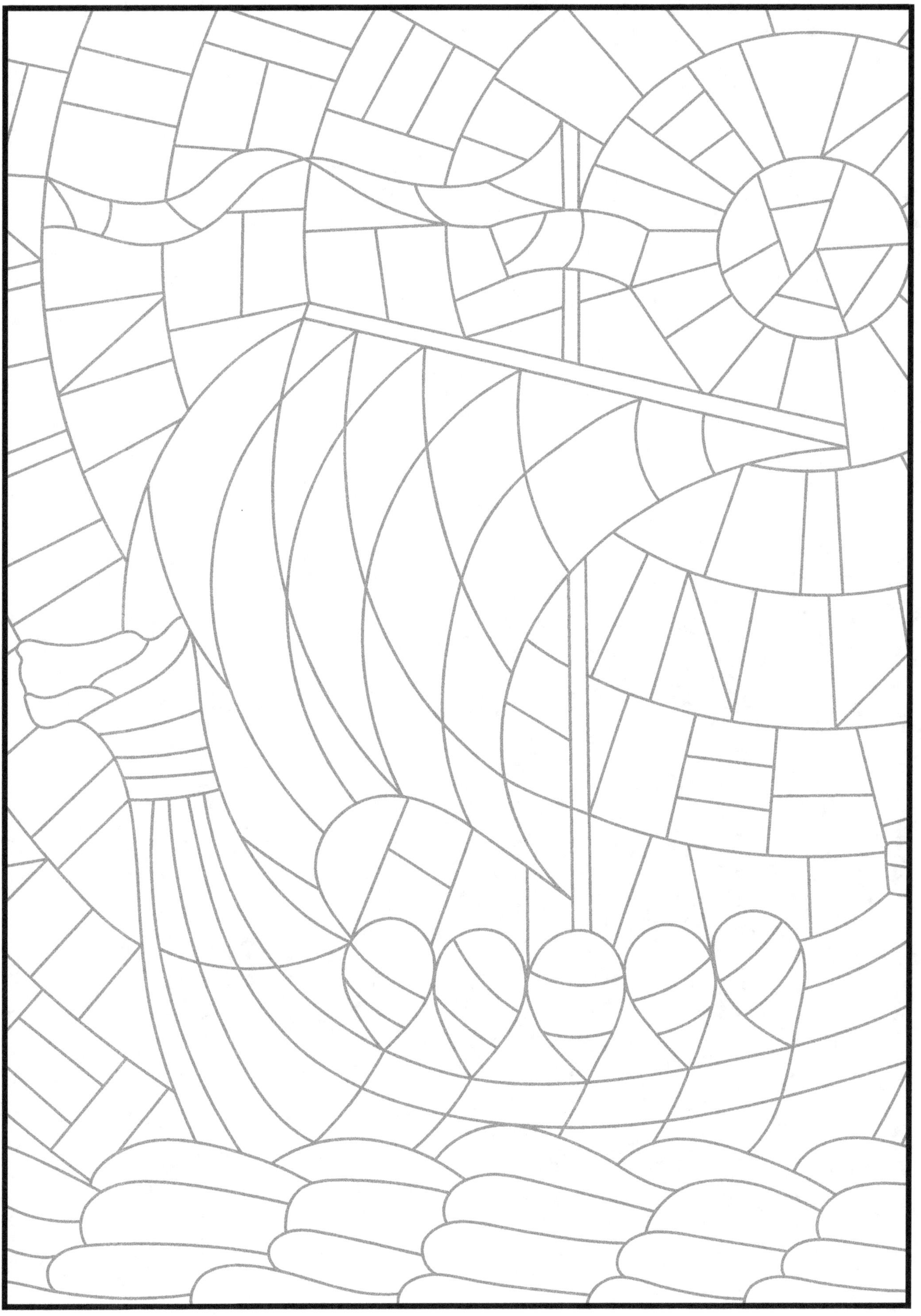

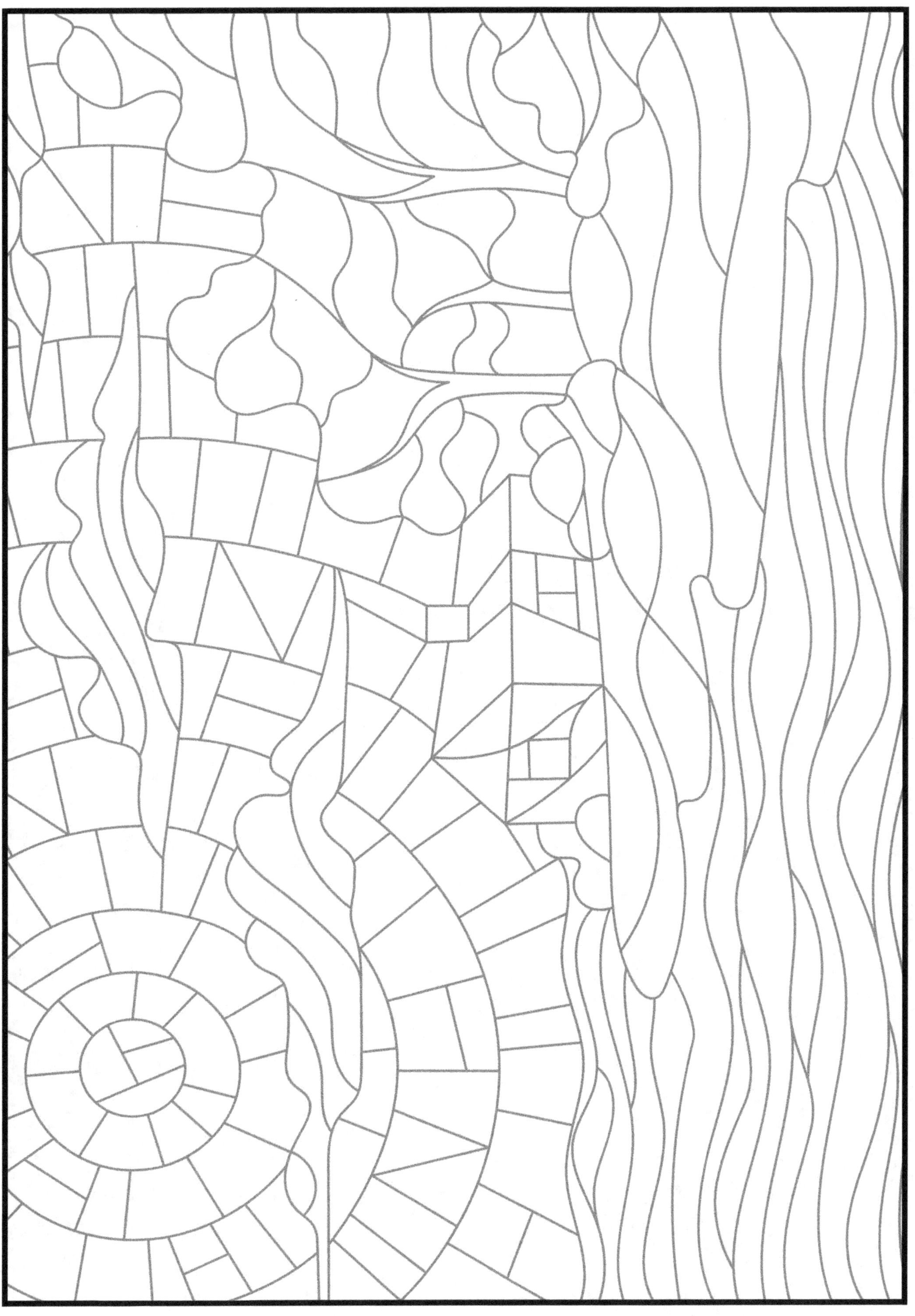

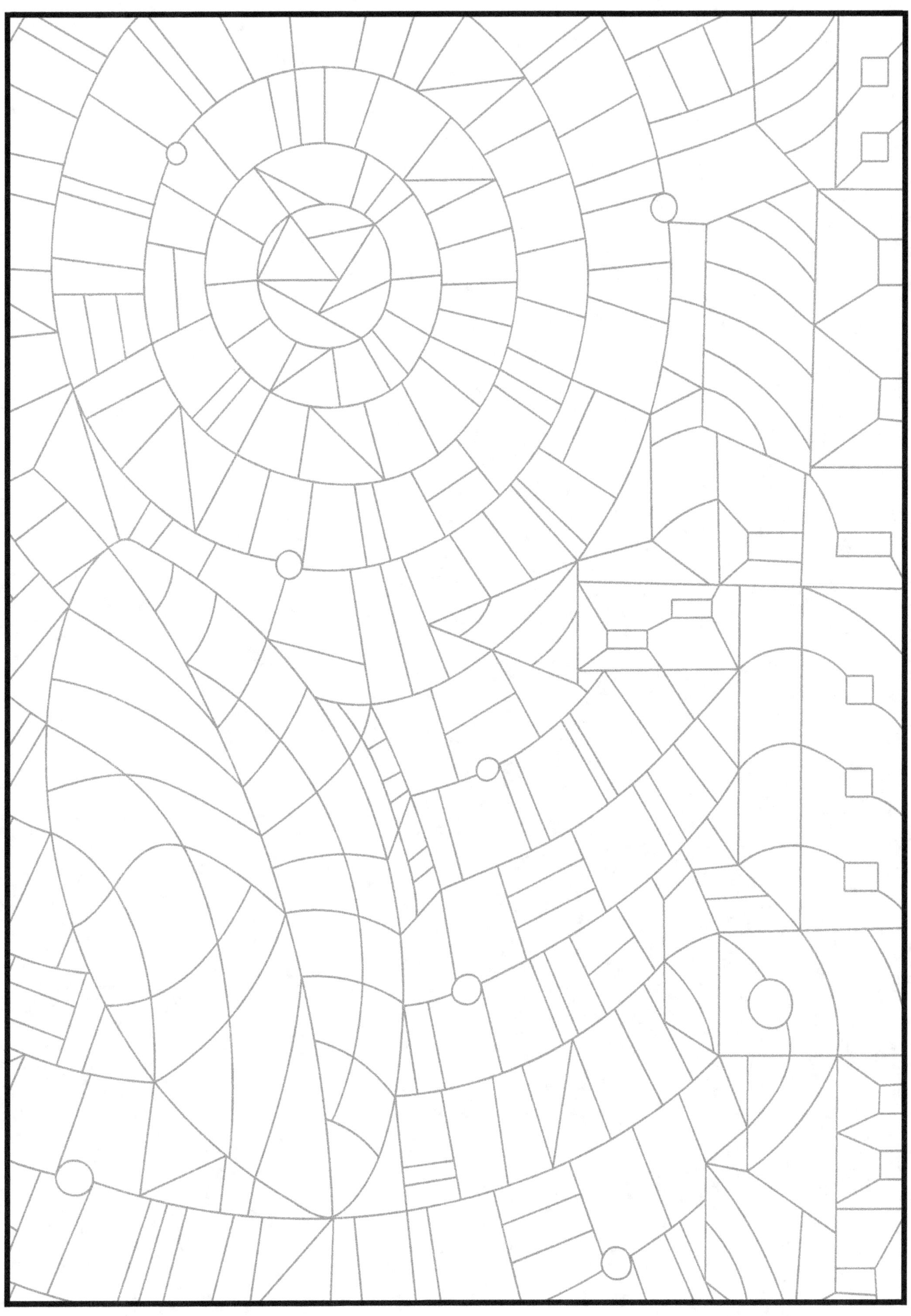

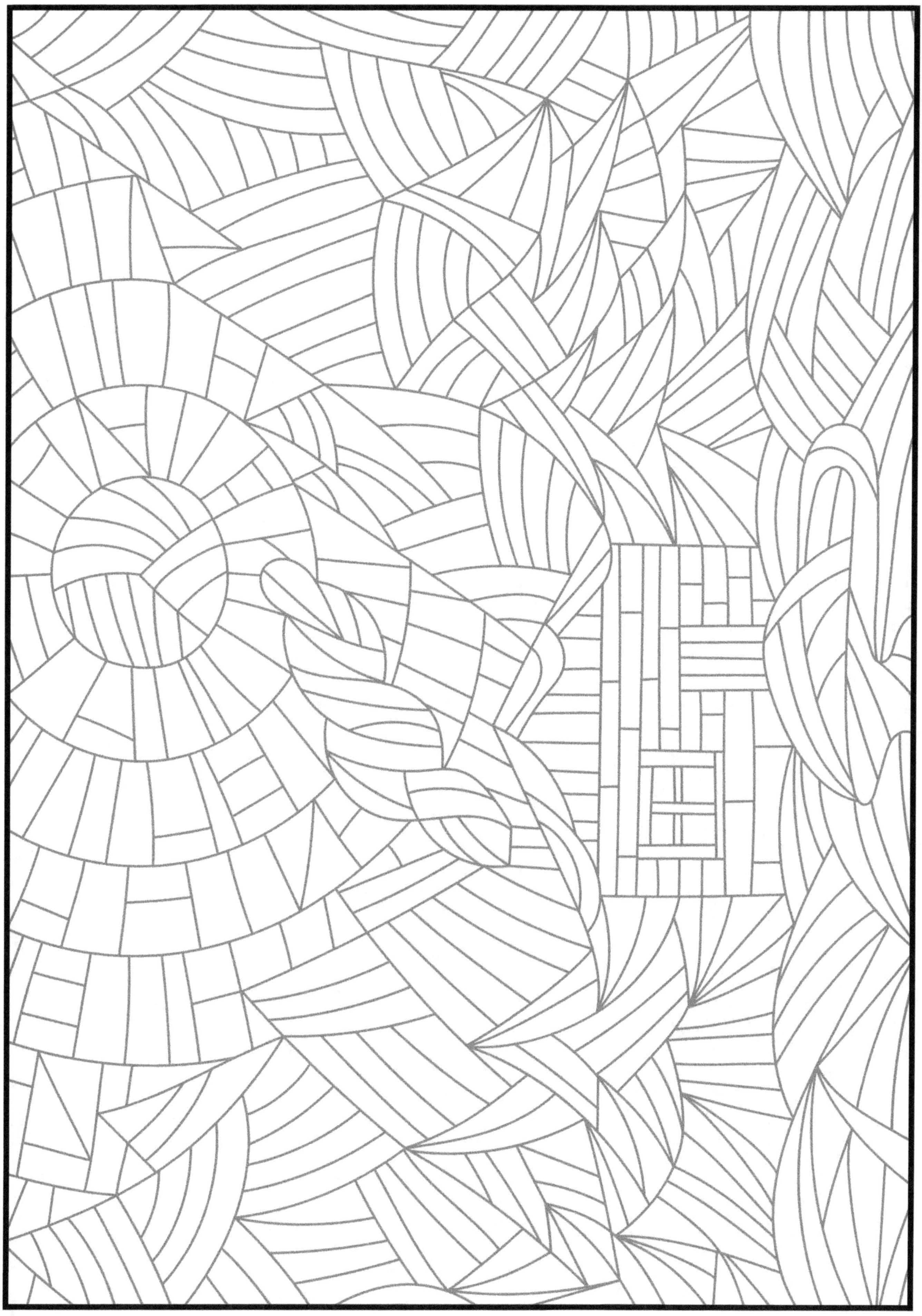

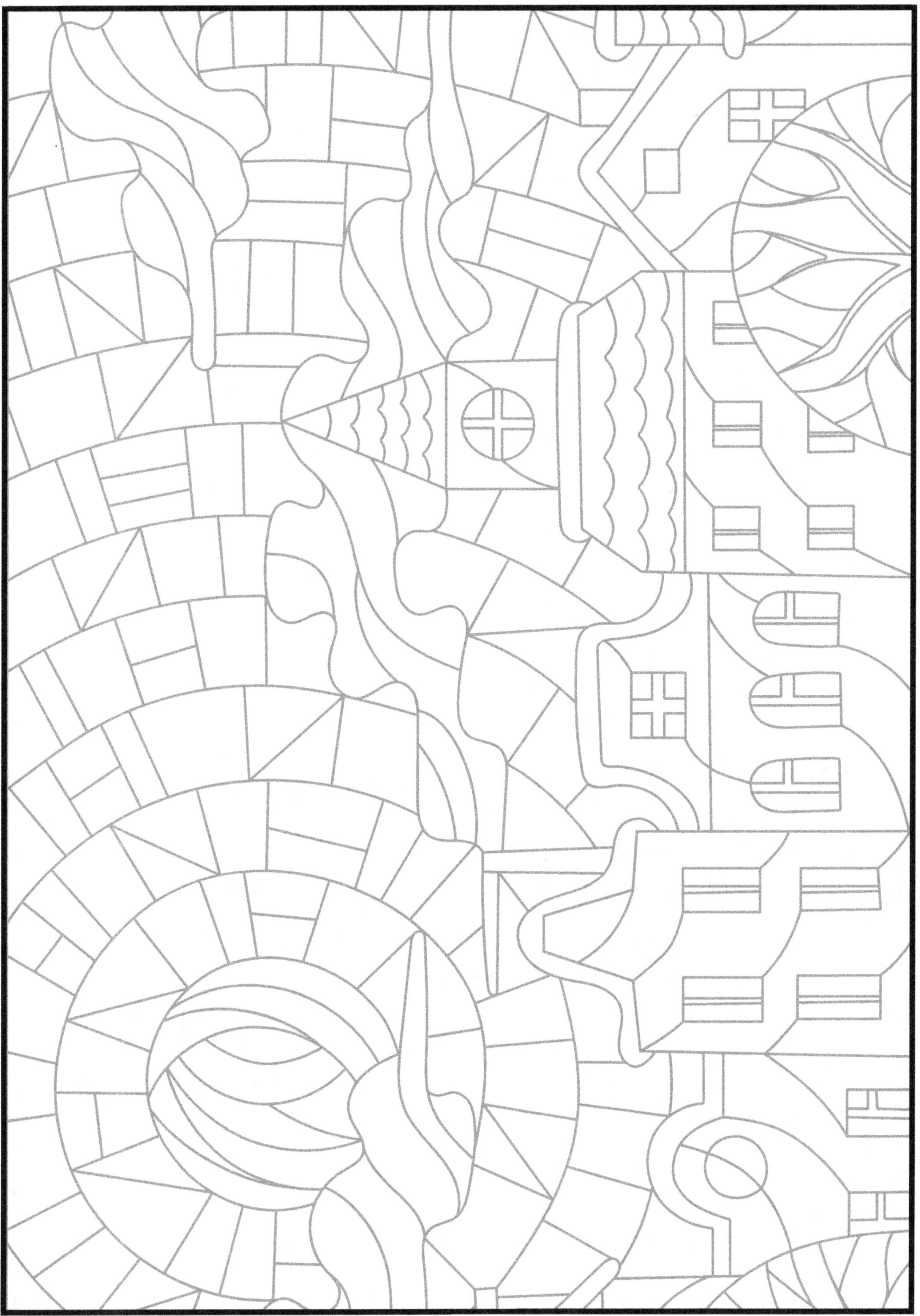

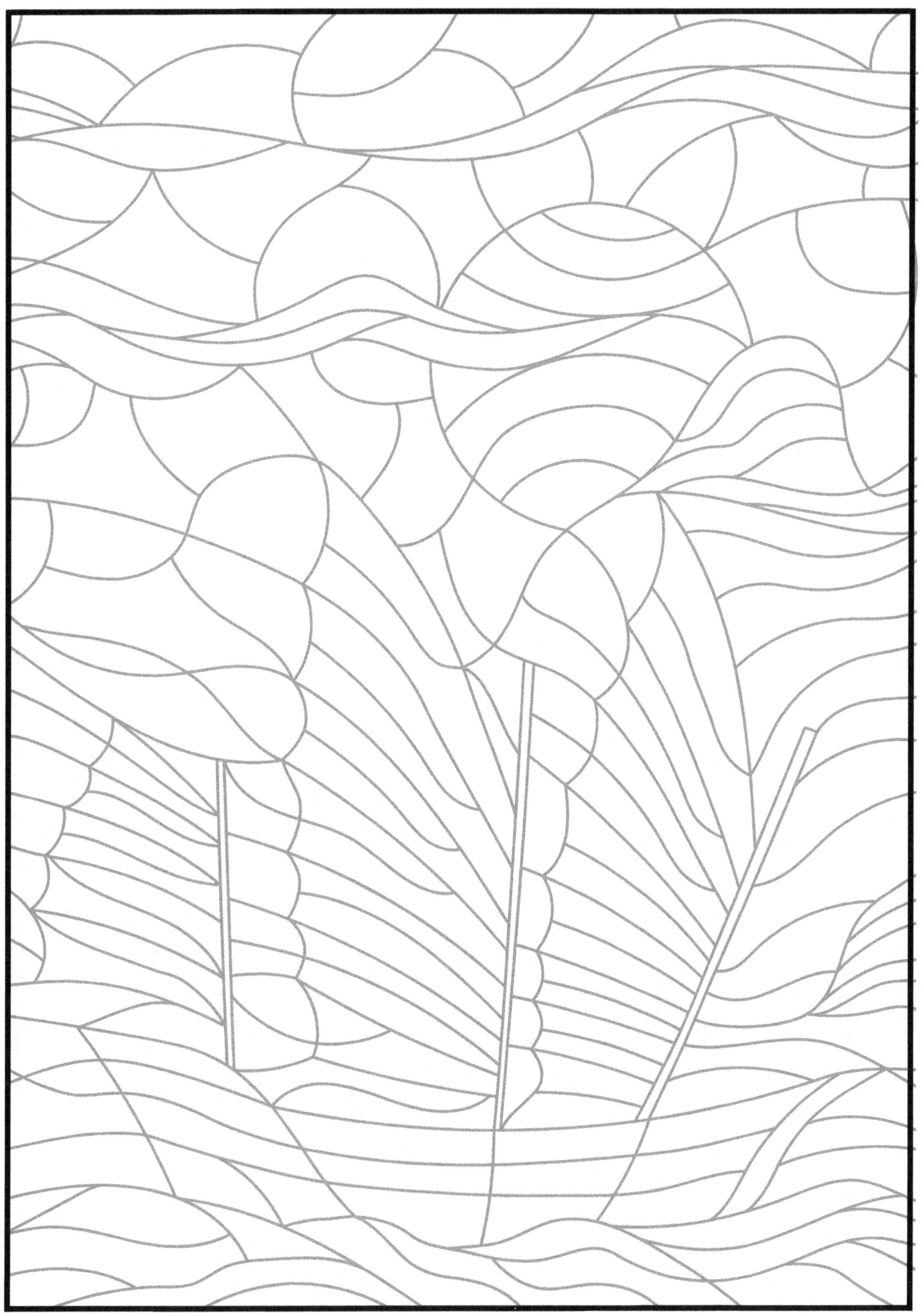

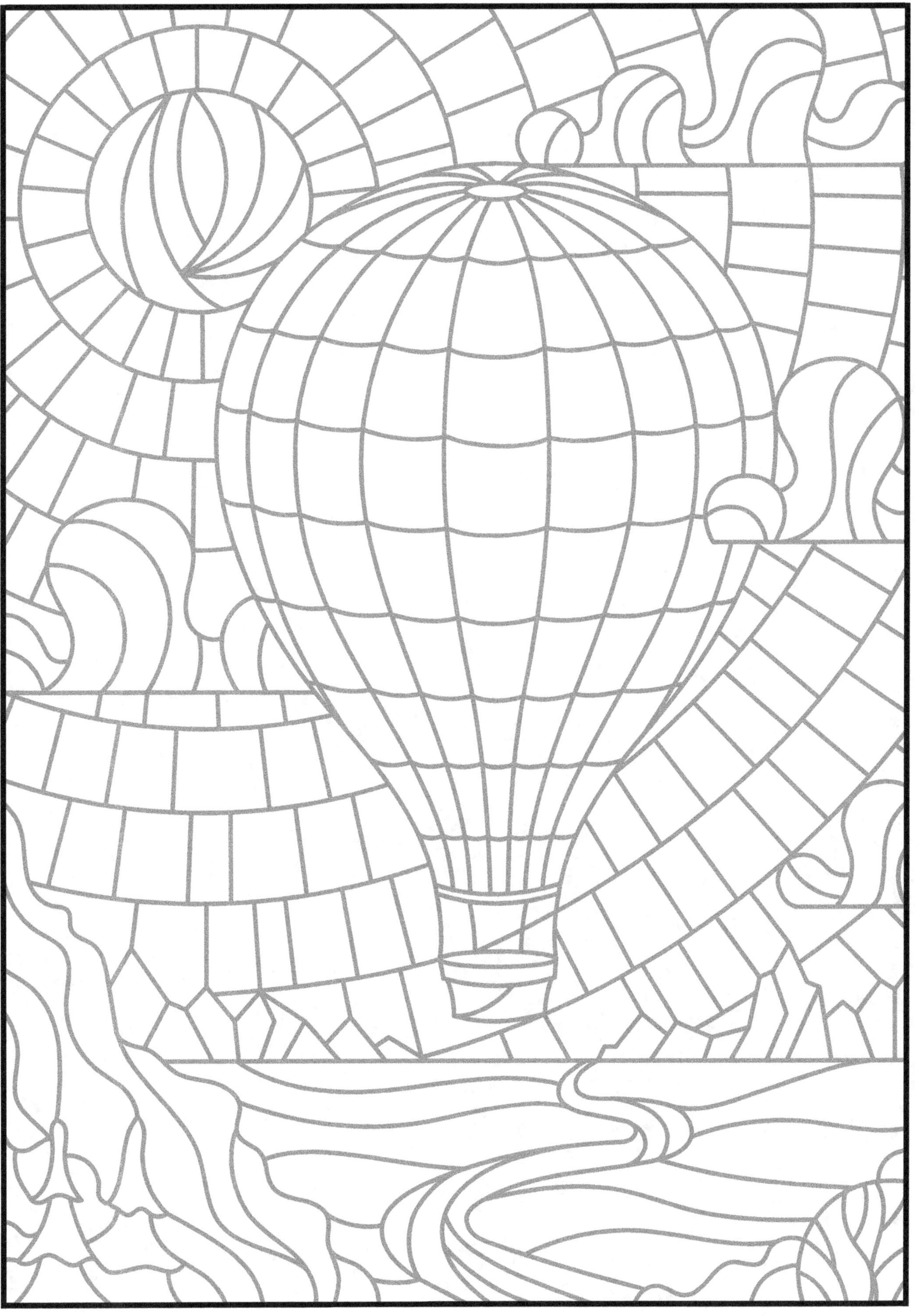

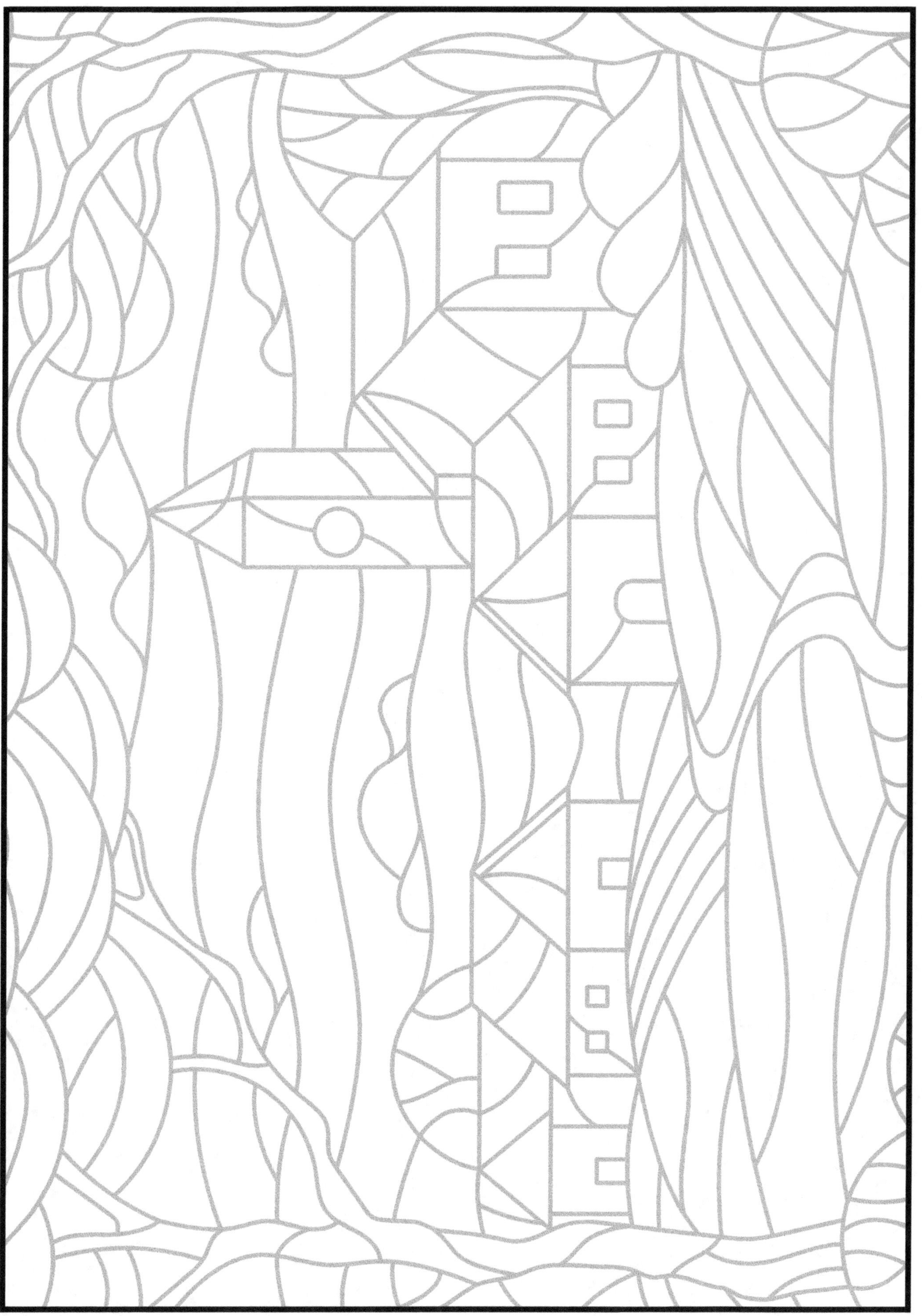

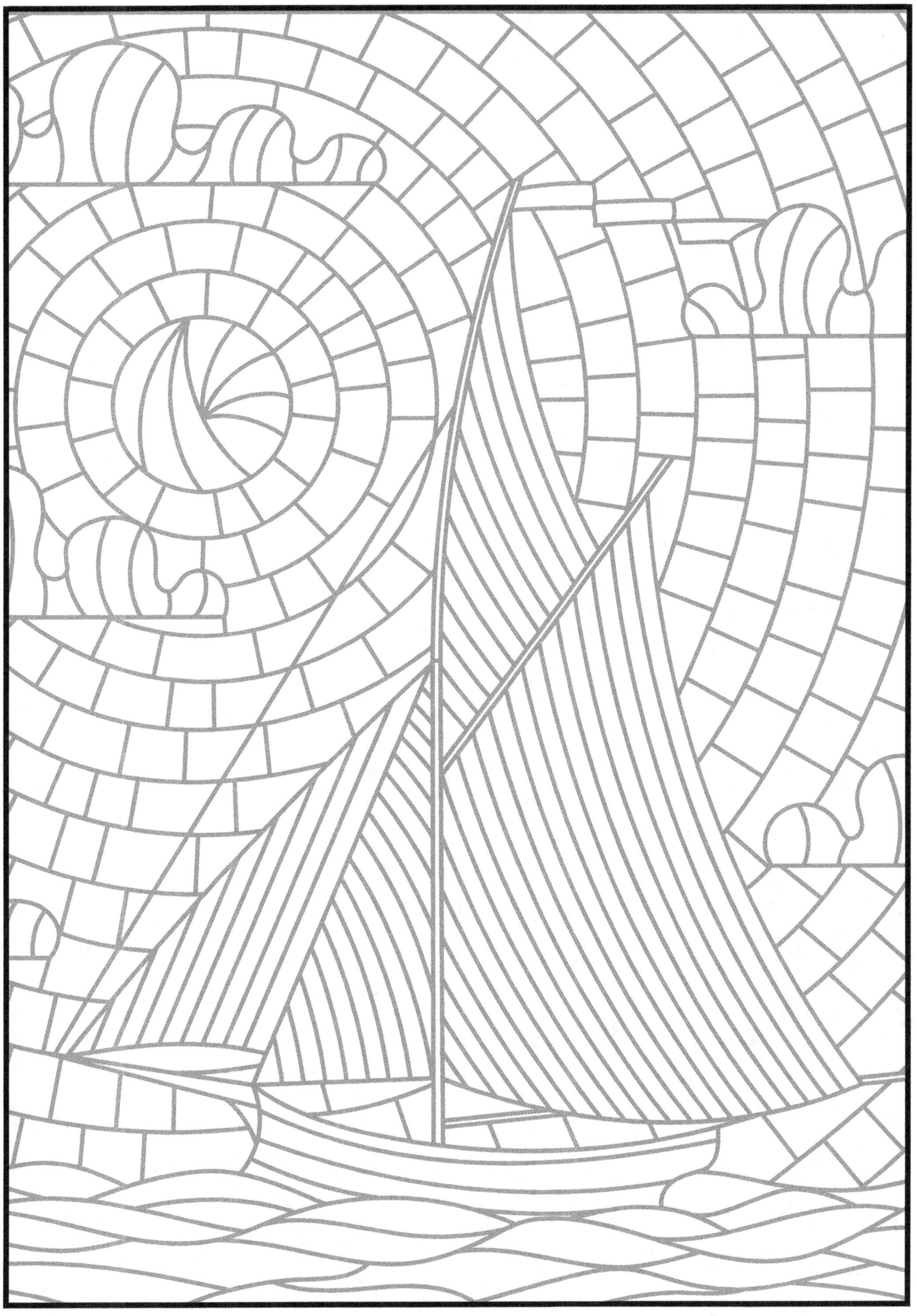

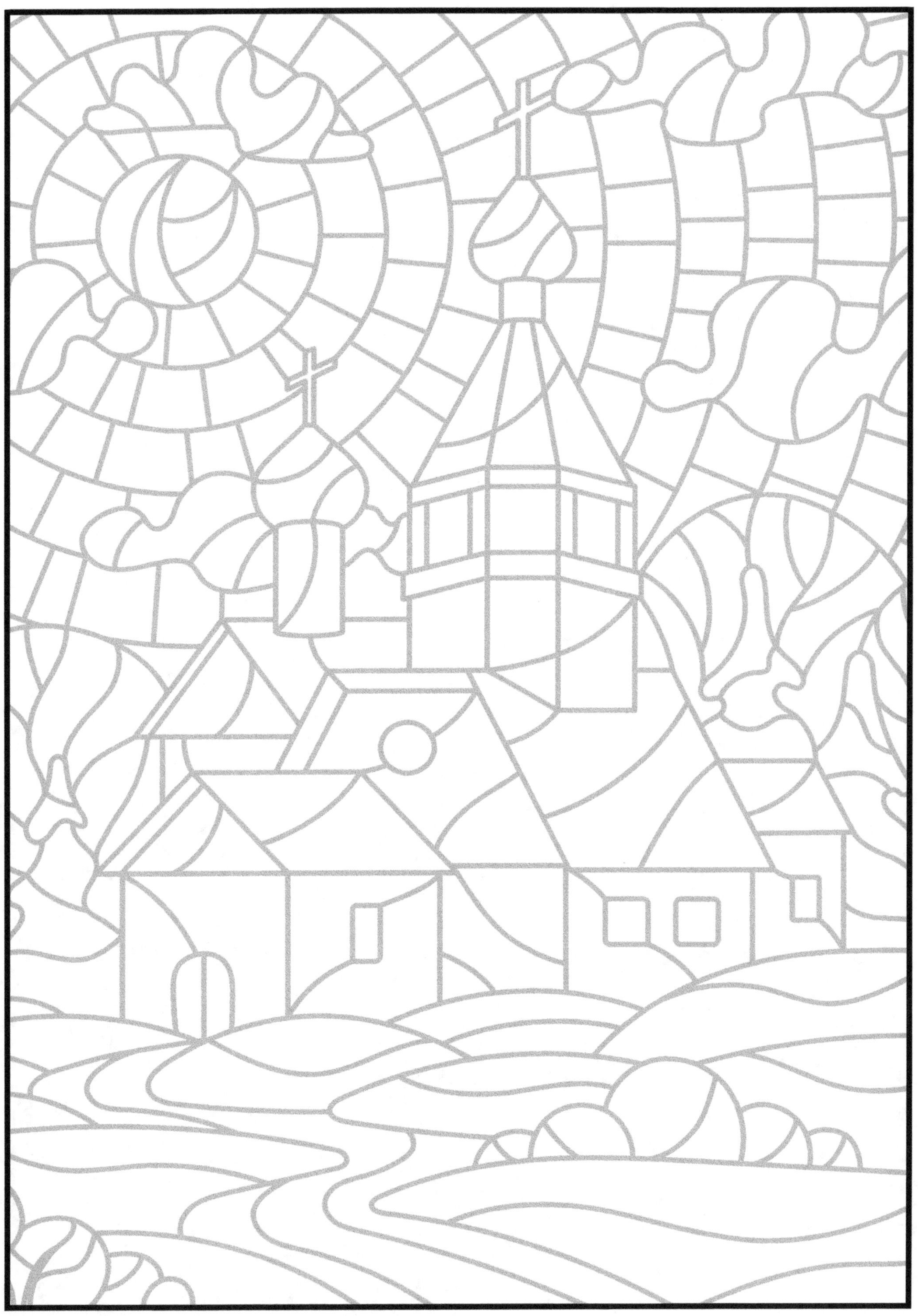

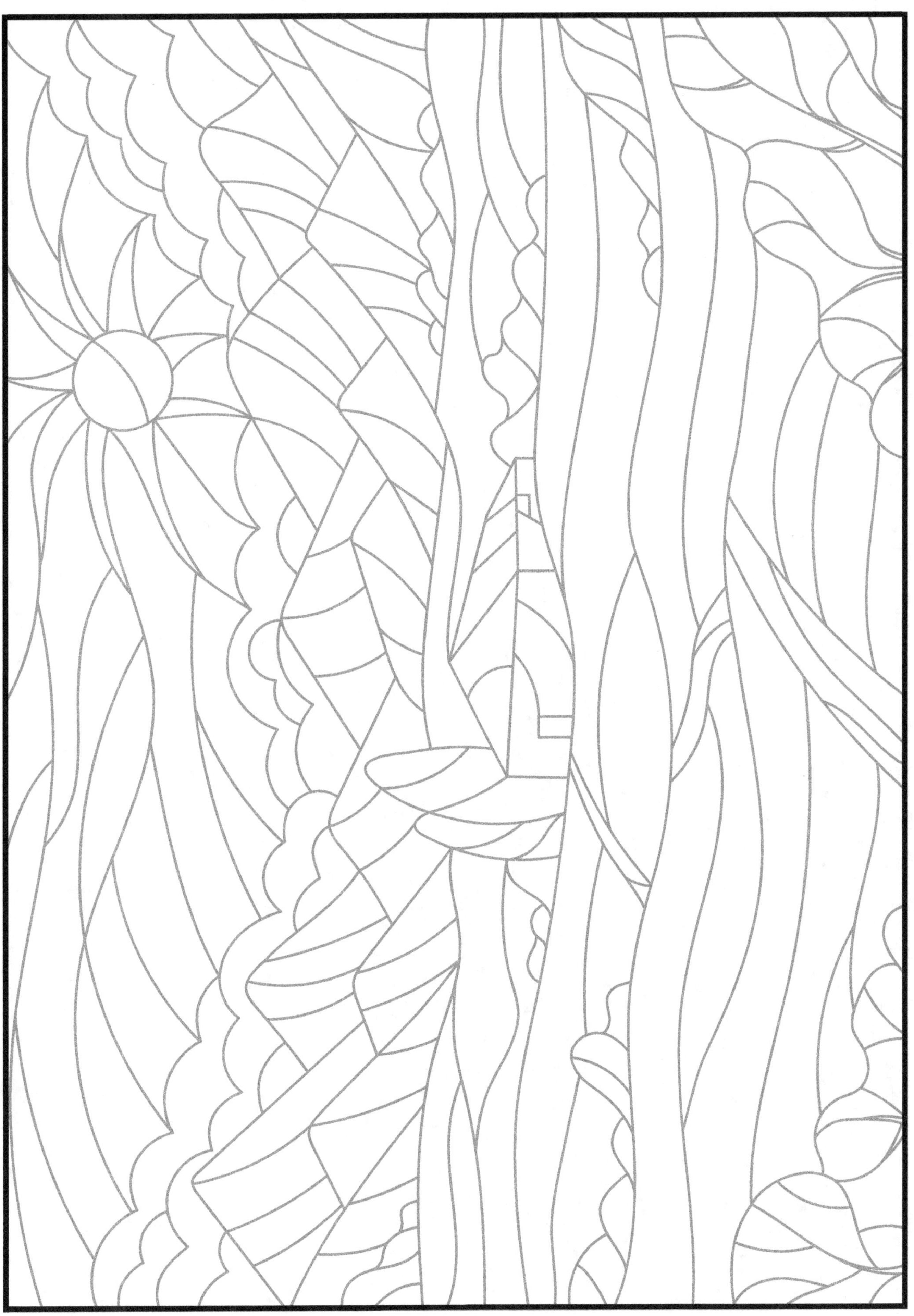

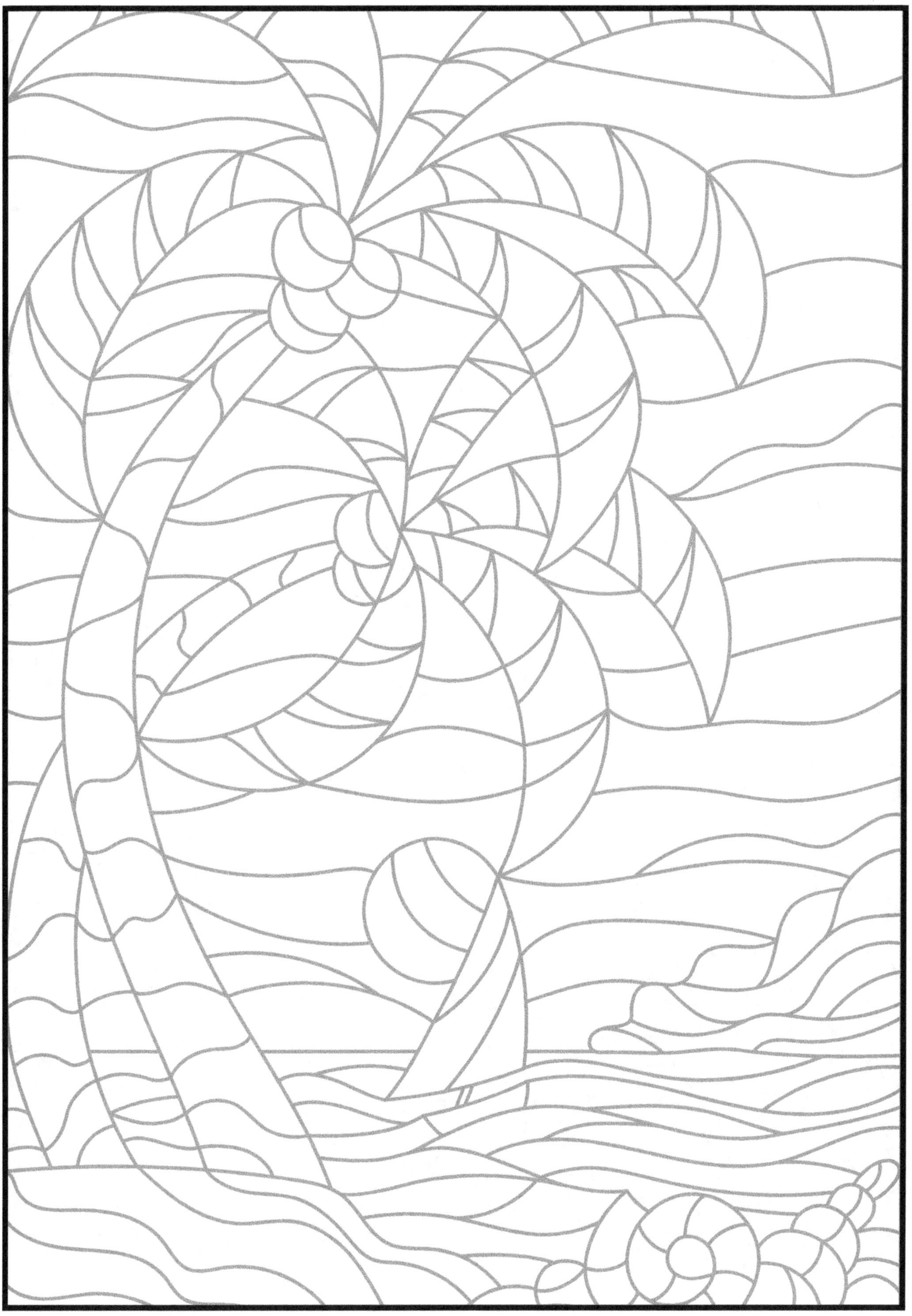

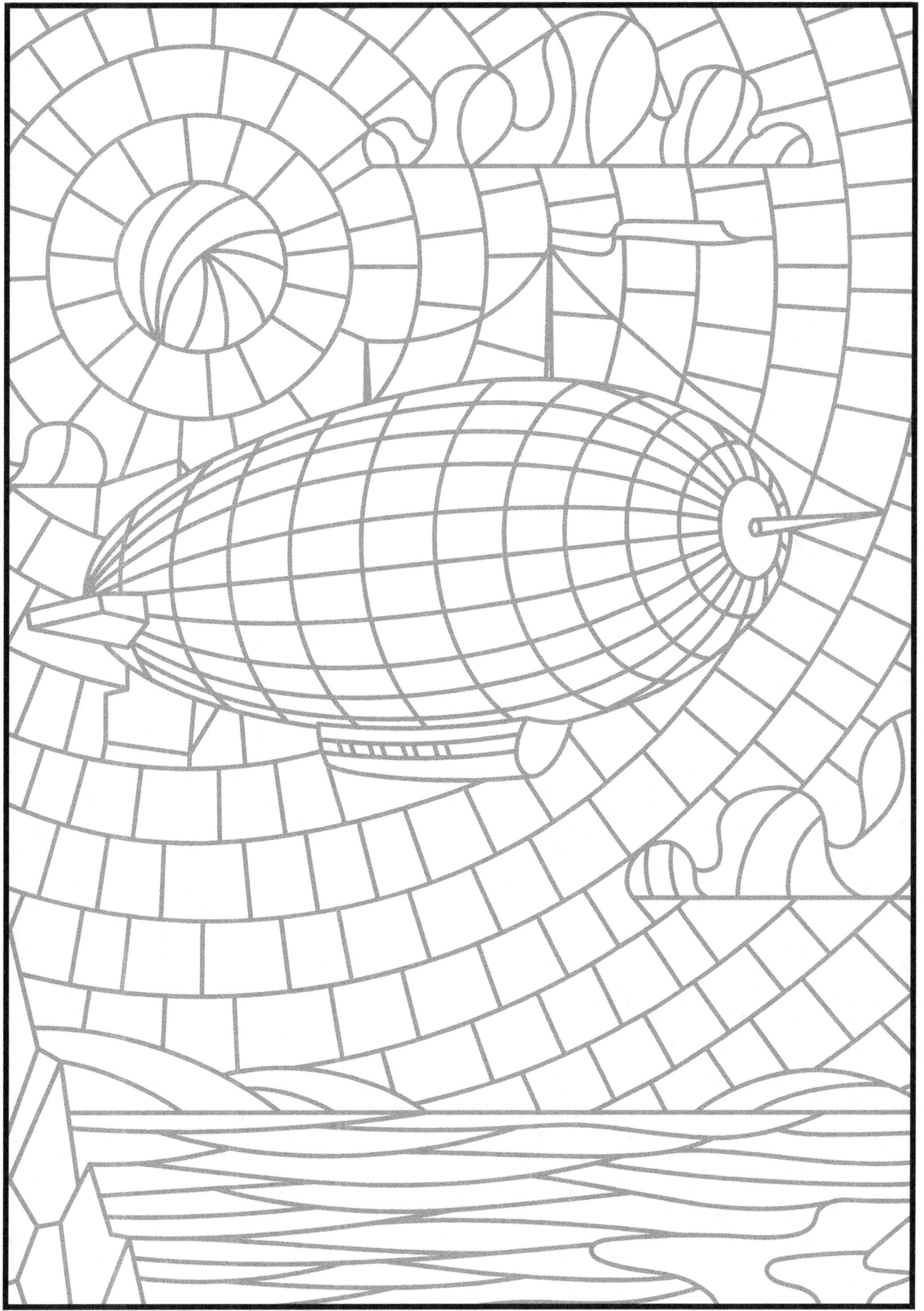

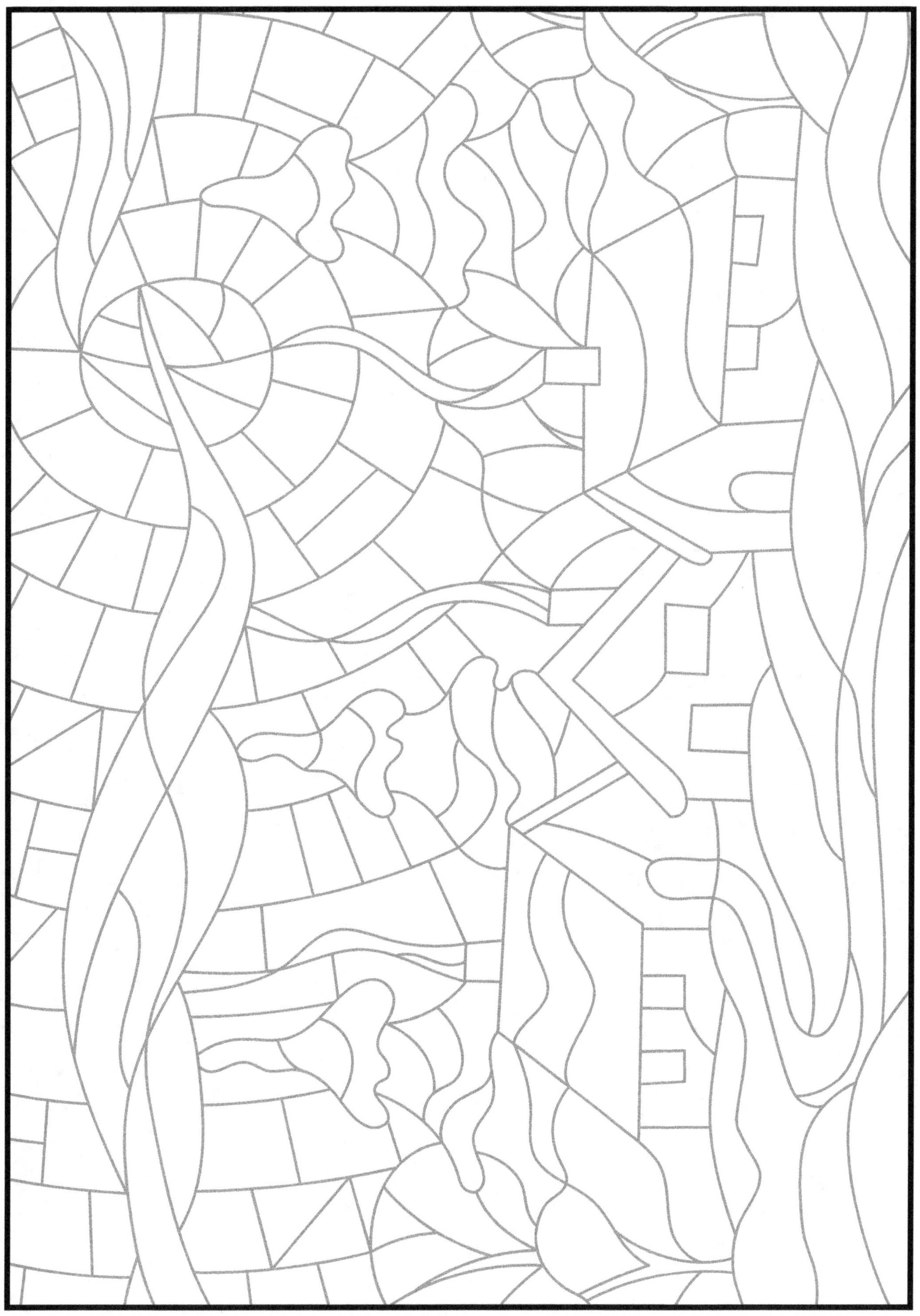

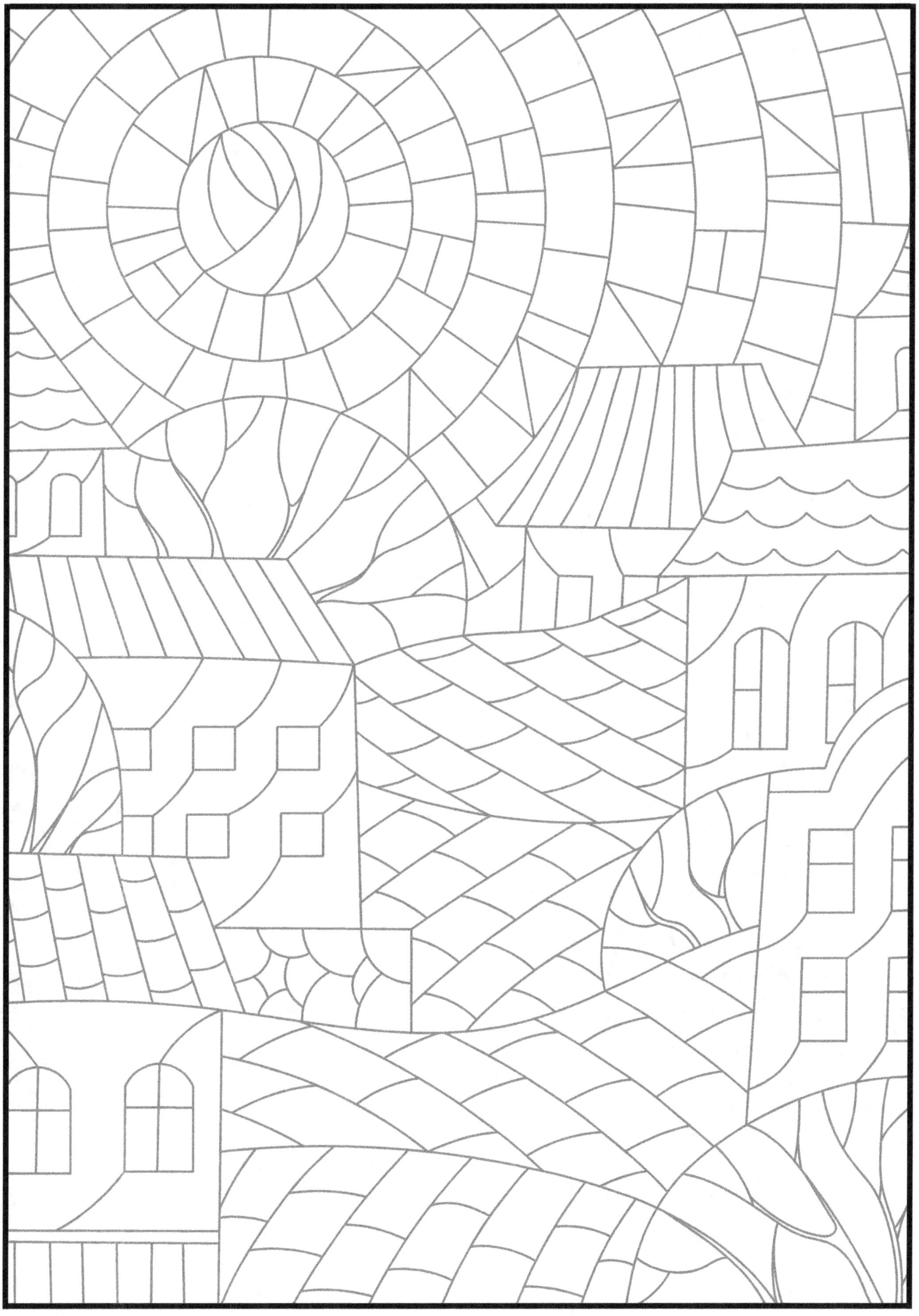

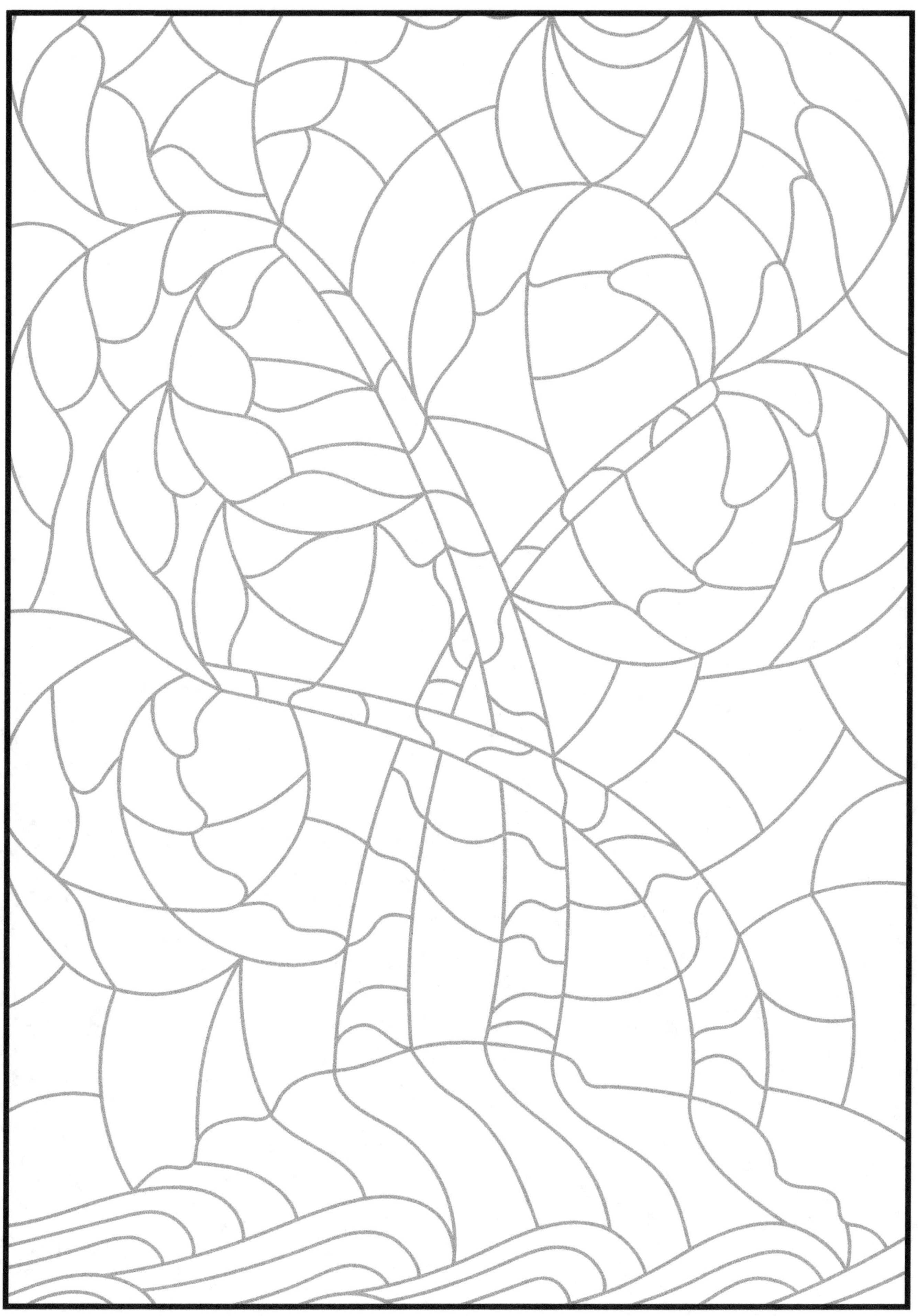

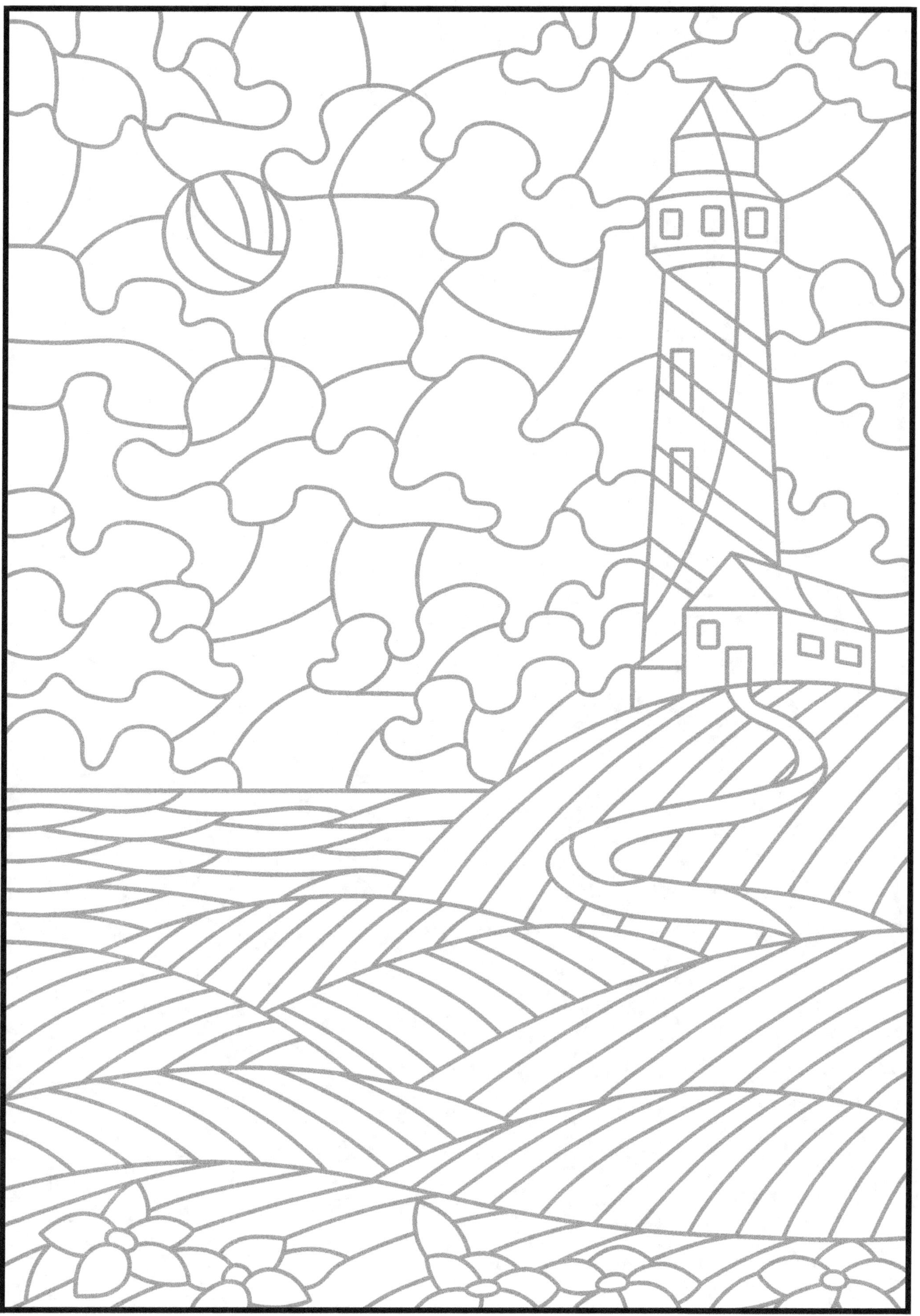

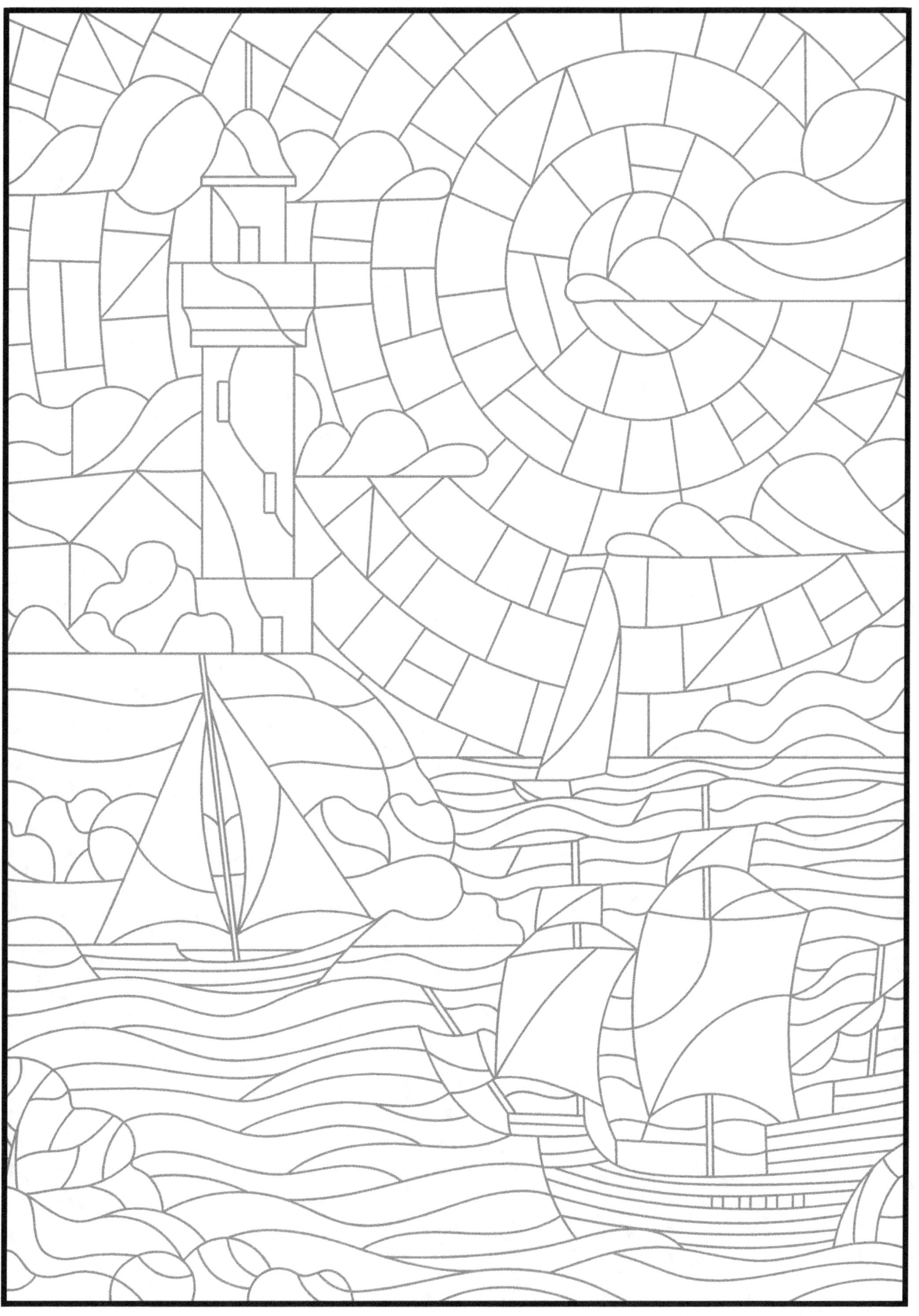

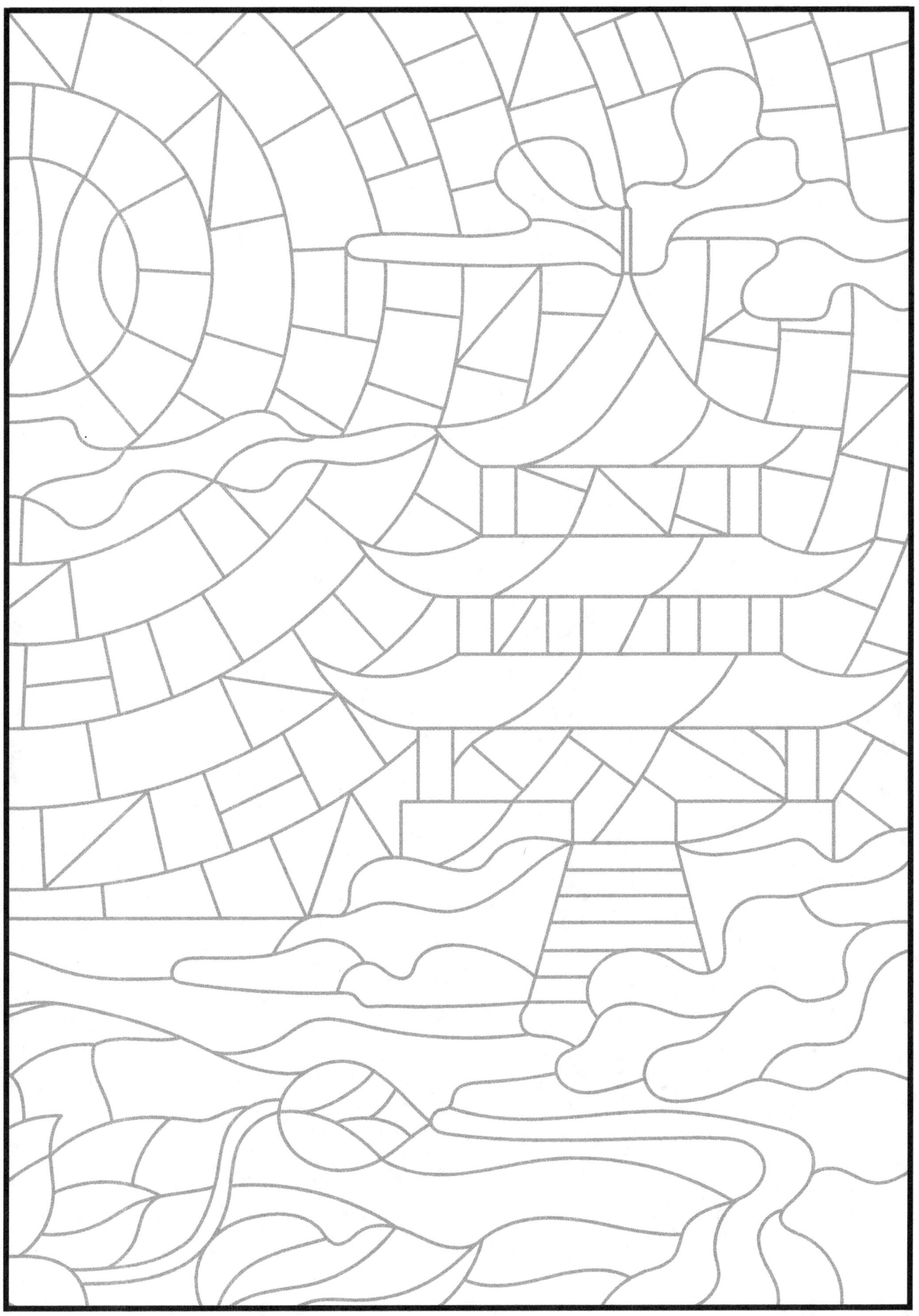

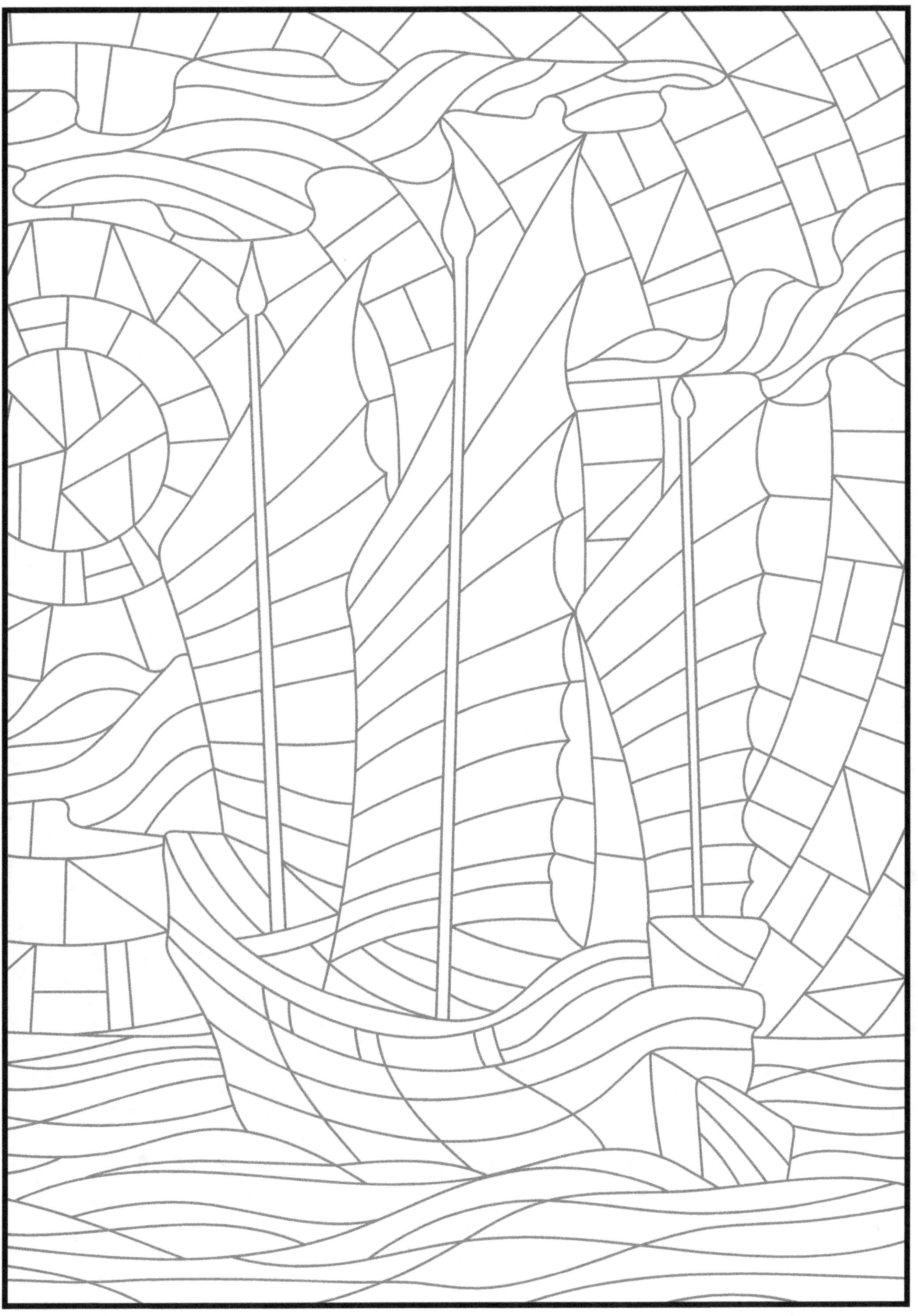

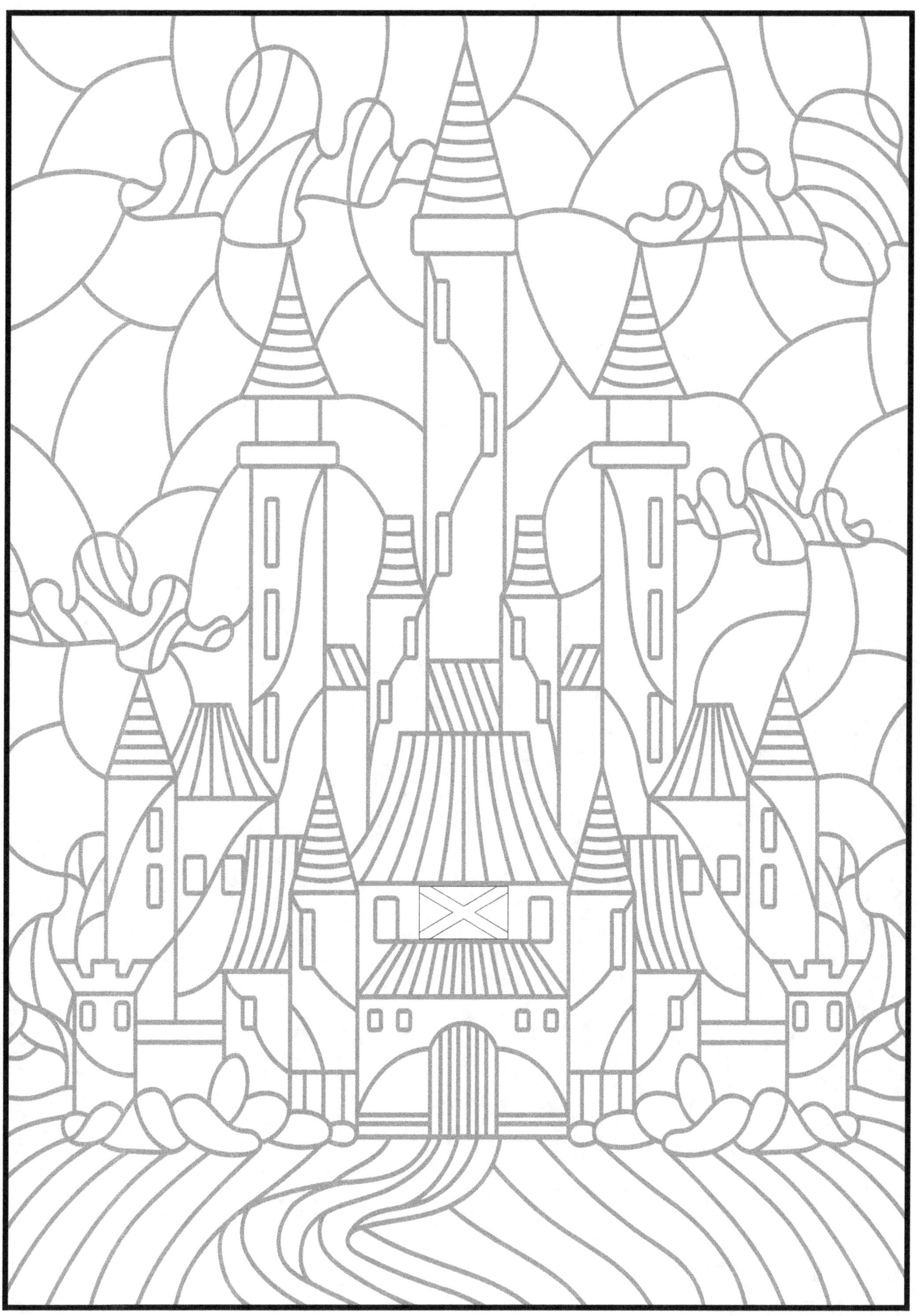

www.ingramcontent.com/pod-product-compliance
Lightning Source LLC
Chambersburg PA
CBHW080352030726
47598CB00009B/2714